Canada

Front cover: A Kwakwaka'wakw totem pole depicting a thunderbird, British Columbia

Right: Canadian moose

TOP 10 ATTRACTIONS

Toronto • From fine dining to fine art, the delights of urban life can be found in Canada's largest city, home of the impressive CN Tower *(page 45)*

Lake Louise in Banff National Park • The area's dramatic mountain and lake scenery is simply dazzling *(page 185)*

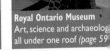

Niagara Falls • This natural wonder deserves to be seen close up *(page 62)*

Royal Ontario Museum • Art, science and archaeology all under one roof *(page 59)*

Wildlife • Glorious viewing in its natural habitat *(page 213)*

Vancouver • Mountains and sea form a lovely backdrop to this cultured, laid-back city *(page 155)*

The great outdoors • Explore the country's vast open spaces *(page 211)*

Montréal • The largest city in the French-speaking province of Québec *(page 87)*

Québec City • More French than Montréal, this small city is a captivating slice of Europe in North America *(page 111)*

The Rocky Mountains • Magnificent scenery on a truly grand scale *(page 180)*

A PERFECT TOUR

Days 1–5 Québec

In Québec City, visit the National Battlefields Park and the Musée de la Civilisation, ride the Lévis ferry, imbibe at Château Frontenac's St-Laurent Bar, and try rabbit at Le Lapin Sauté. Take the train to Montréal on Day 3. Explore romantic Old Montréal, the free-spirited Latin Quarter, and Mont-Royal Parc. Board an evening train to Ottawa.

Days 8–9 Best of Toronto

Get a lofty perspective at the CN Tower, then stroll around downtown, enjoying its architectural contrasts. Bustling St Lawrence Market is perfect for lunch. Weather permitting, explore Harbourfront Centre or Toronto Islands. Alternatively, shop at the Eaton Centre or along West Queen West. On Day 9, Chinatown and Kensington Market offer plenty to see and eat, before visiting Royal Ontario Museum, then a drink in the Park Hyatt's Roof Lounge.

Days 10–12 Niagara

Take a leisurely drive, following the magnificent Niagara Escarpment and the Wine Route. Stay a night in Niagara Falls, dining above the illuminated falls. Head to Niagara-on-the-Lake – a short distance, but plenty to see. Relax over dinner or catch a play at the Shaw Festival.

Days 6–7 The nation's capital

Begin by touring Parliament Hill. Musts on Ottawa's museum circuit include the Canadian Museum of Civilisation, the National Gallery of Canada and the Canadian War Museum. Shop around lively ByWard Market, and meander along the Rideau Canal. Take an evening train to Toronto.

OF CANADA

Day 15 | Icefields Parkway

Take your time driving the spectacular Icefields Parkway. Many walking trails from it lead to secluded canyons and waterfalls. Stop by Columbia Icefields Interpretive Centre and ride the Ice Explorer onto the Athabasca Glacier's slopes, then continue to Jasper.

Days 18–21 | Sky high

Take the Peak2Peak gondola, and have lunch on a mountaintop patio. The next day, ride the Sea to Sky train, beside Howe Sound, to Vancouver. Explore Stanley Park, stop by English Bay's Sylvia Hotel for a beer, and visit UBC's campus and the Museum of Anthropology. For the ultimate fish and chips, try Go Fish.

Days 13–14 | Calgary

Fly from Toronto to Calgary. Dine on trendy Stephen Avenue or 4th Street. Depart early for Banff to ride the Sulphur Mountain gondola, or soak in Upper Hot Springs pool. Continue to Lake Louise for the night. Hike around the glacial lake beneath Victoria Glacier, and visit historic Fairmont Chateau Lake Louise.

Days 16–17 | Riding the Rocky Mountaineer

Take an unforgettable train journey through the Yellowhead Pass, past Mount Robson and Rocky Mountain Trench, into BC. Stay overnight in Quesnel. Delight in sweeping views of Fraser Canyon, Seton Lake and Anderson Lake, en route to Whistler, before reaching the rolling hills of the Cariboo Plateau, the Fraser Canyon and lush Pemberton Valley.

CONTENTS

40

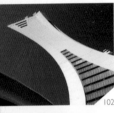

102

87

226

212

106

INTRODUCTION

Canada is an immense country, crowning the North American continent with an intriguing combination of sophisticated urban living and indomitable wilderness. The advanced industrial society that stretches along the border with the US looks out of its back door onto inexhaustible rainforests, a powerful network of rivers and lakes, and mountain ranges reaching up into the Arctic tundra.

Enduring Arctic Image

To those with only a dim notion of the place, Canada is a land of year-round snow, polar bears and Inuit peoples, of earmuffed lumberjacks huddled around campfires with Arctic wolves howling in the distance. Urban legend tells of tourists driving over the Canadian border with skis on the car roof in July – they'd have a long way to go before they found any snow. Yet the Arctic image still persists.

For most Canadians, the Far North starts beyond the treeline in their most populous provinces: Québec and Ontario. This is the beginning of the great glacial plateau known as the Canadian Shield, which stretches in a wide arc along the shores of the Hudson Bay, across northern Manitoba and Saskatchewan to the Northwest Territories. The terrain is rough and rocky, strewn with swamps and lakes as far as the bleak tundra.

Beyond this landscape lies the vast, unyielding Arctic permafrost. The name of a national park says it all: Auyuittuq, 'the place that never melts'. But underneath the ice is gold, silver, lead, uranium, oil and gas; Canada's First Nations and Inuit are vying with the federal government for control of these riches.

A vast 'village'

The name Canada is thought to derive from a word in the Algonquin Indian language: *kanata*, which means 'village'.

A riot of autumnal colours on show in Nova Scotia

The futurist architecture of downtown Toronto

Tradition and Modernity

Canada's cities make excellent launching pads from which to explore the great outdoors. They also provide ample illustrations of Canadian paradoxes. In a typical suburban driveway, for example, you are more than likely to see the latest expensive car and a canoe parked side by side. Montréal synthesises Canada's special mix of New World modernity and Old World charm, with massive modern and post-modern skyscrapers alongside gracious grey-stone mansions.

For many North Americans, the unashamed quaintness of old Québec City offers a first taste of all things French. Similarly, the dynamic city of Toronto offers Europeans a gleaming Canadian version of America – 'cleaner and nicer', say the locals, with no visible trace of modesty. The federal capital, Ottawa, is known for its superb museums and a thriving high-tech industry, as well as its major 'industry': government bureaucracy. The disarming brash-ness of Calgary reminds many visitors of Texas, while Vancouver's scintillating location between the Pacific Ocean and the Coastal Mountains gives the city a relaxed elegance all its own.

Rich Resources

Beyond the cities, Canada still talks a pioneering language: challenge, high risk, adventure, remote frontiers to chart, empty wastelands yet to conquer. Canada's landmass could swallow the US, with France, Belgium and the Netherlands thrown in for good measure. The forests alone cover an area six times the size of France. Yet the population is nine times less than that of its North American neighbour.

The transcontinental railways, Canadian Pacific and Canadian National, made it possible to cross this giant country by the end of the 19th century. Now, VIA Rail is Canada's passenger rail service provider, and it, together with the Trans-Canada Highway – which stretches from Victoria, BC to St. John's, Newfoundland – are vital arteries of national unity.

In the east, tough, stoical Newfoundland is whipped by the winds from the Atlantic. It draws its charm from the fishing villages huddled around the rugged coast. The province includes Labrador, snowbound for more than half the year. The Maritime provinces – Nova Scotia, Prince Edward Island and New Brunswick – are a shade more sheltered; their hinterland dotted with sleepy farms, orchards and pine forests. For the world market, Atlantic salmon is king, but for gourmets, Nova Scotia's lobster is without equal.

Crisscrossing Québec from the St Lawrence Seaway to the Hudson Bay are cascading, rock-strewn rivers. They provide hydroelectric power for use both at home – where Canadians refer to electricity as 'hydro' – and in the US. The thick forests of the Laurentian Mountains still furnish pulp, paper and construction timber, despite continued clearing for more and more ski resorts.

On the Rideau Canal, Ottawa

Ontario is Canada's hub. It shares four of the five Great Lakes with the US, but keeps for itself the best access to the Niagara Falls. With manufacturing, agriculture, forestry and mining being its major activities, the province dominates Canada's industry and commerce. The land is blessed with lush cattle pastures and rich seams of nickel, uranium, iron, copper, gold and silver. Ontario is also the home of the national capital, Ottawa, a city that originally evolved – under the name of Bytown – as part of the defence of British North America against the US.

Breadbasket not only to Canada but also to much of the rest of the world, the wheatfields of the Prairie provinces of Manitoba and Saskatchewan stretch to infinity. The Prairies continue into Alberta, but the cattle ranches and oil industry in the foothills of the Rocky Mountains set the region apart as the beginning of Canada's west, home of the rodeo and the Calgary Stampede.

Calgary Stampede

For British Columbia (BC), the Rockies are more of an obstacle than a link to the rest of Canada. The province seems happy to nestle up to the Pacific Ocean with the mildest weather in the country in its southern portion. The Pacific is an abundant provider of salmon. Vineyards and orchards line the valleys of the interior.

Although no longer the lifeblood of British Columbia's economy, timber continues to be the province's major export. The lumberjack's legendary image was created here in forests covering two-thirds of the land;

they are also the cradle of the Douglas fir, the most majestic of all the evergreens.

The Canadians

And what of the Canadians themselves? Their quest for an identity continues, as they are torn between the insistent influence of the American culture across the border and the more remote but strong emotional pull of the Old World. In May, everywhere except Québec celebrates Victoria Day, a statutory holiday, named in honour of Queen Victoria's birthday; now it is simply

Victoria Day celebrations

a celebration of the current sovereign's official birthday. The city of Victoria, capital of British Columbia, is considered by some Brits to be more 'English' than England, while neighbouring Vancouver looks down its coast to Seattle and San Francisco rather than back east to fellow Canadian cities. With the huge increase in their ethnic populations in recent years, both Montréalers and Torontonians are as interested in Hong Kong and Shanghai as they are in London and Paris.

National identity is further diluted by fierce regional rivalries. The more recently prosperous west is eager to assert itself over the traditional power bases of Ontario and Québec. The perennially poorer Atlantic provinces are wary of all their neighbours, while, with the establishment of the new province of Nunavut, Canada's aboriginal peoples are impatient to obtain the privileges of full provincial status in the Yukon and the western part of the Northwest Territories.

French-speaking Canadians represent around 21 percent of the national population, concentrated mostly in Québec, but with important minorities in Ontario, New Brunswick and Manitoba.

Their separate language and ongoing struggle for a 'distinct society', in reality a distinct nationality separate from Canada, have given them a stronger sense of identity, especially apparent in contemporary literature and cinema.

Canadians who are not French-speaking include 670,500 Canadians of German extraction, 741,000 Italians, 300,500 Ukrainians, more than 1,135,000 Chinese, and hundreds of thousands of Indians, Filipinos, Portuguese, Poles, Vietnamese and Arabic speakers from around the world. While maintaining their religious and ethnic traditions, many groups have their own newspapers and radio and television stations, and have brought from their 'old country' a spicy alternative to the formerly pervasive Anglo-Saxon cuisine. Prime examples include Vancouver's Chinatown, Toronto's trattorias, and Montréal's Jewish delicatessens. The 28 percent of the population who do claim British origin are quick to let you know if they are Scots, Welsh or Irish, rather than English. The Scots in particular are proud of the Macdonald, Mackenzie and other families who provided the first prime ministers, and dominated banking and railway management as well as the fur and timber trades.

Niagara Falls

In the end, despite their regional and ethnic rivalries, most Canadians remain united by their underlying tolerance of diversity – and by their love of the enduring challenge of that great, and still largely untamed land of theirs.

Facts and Figures

Canada is constantly evolving, and some figures quoted here are subject to change. For the latest statistics, visit www.statcan.ca.

Geography: Canada covers 9,970,610 sq km (2,991,183 sq miles). From Ellesmere Island in the Arctic, south across Hudson Bay to Lake Erie's Middle Island, a crow would have to fly 4,634km (2,878 miles). Its east–west trip from Cape Spear, Newfoundland, to the Yukon-Alaska border covers 5,154km (3,200 miles). Canada and the US share the Great Lakes of Ontario, Erie, Huron, Michigan and Superior. Canada's rivers include the Mackenzie and Yukon in the north, the St Lawrence flowing from Lake Ontario to the Atlantic, the Saskatchewan through the prairies, and the Columbia and Fraser to the Pacific. The Western Cordillera, formed by the Rocky Mountains and the Coast Range, contains the highest peak, Mt Logan (5,951m/19,524ft), in the Yukon.

Population: 34,108,800 (close to 1,200,000 of aboriginal ancestry, including 50,500 Inuit); 58% English mother tongue, 22% French, 20% whose mother tongue is neither, including Italian, German and Asian.

Capital: Ottawa, population 1,239,000+.

Major cities: Toronto (5,435,500), Montréal (3,859,300), Vancouver (2,213,500), Edmonton (1,176,300), Calgary (1,242,600), Winnipeg (753,600), Québec City (754,400).

Government: Canada is a constitutional monarchy at the heart of the British Commonwealth, with a governor general appointed by the Queen. The prime minister and cabinet answer to a 308-member House of Commons, elected for a maximum five-year term. The mainly consultative Senate has 105 members appointed on the advice of the prime minister. The 10 provinces have autonomy over education, healthcare, housing and natural resources; the Yukon, the Northwest Territories and Nunavut depend more directly on Ottawa.

Religion: Over the past two decades there has been a growth in non-Christian religions. Catholic 43%; Protestant 29%; Islam 2%; Eastern Orthodox 1.6%; Jewish 1%; Buddhist 1%; Hindu 1%; Sikhism 1%.

A BRIEF HISTORY

Is it history or folklore that suggests St Brendan, a 6th-century monk from Galway, was the first European to reach Canada? The people of Newfoundland, where he is said to have landed, certainly like to think he was. After all, on his return he told of being attacked by insects as big as chickens. 'Of course,' say the Newfies, 'they must have been our giant mosquitoes!'

A more serious claim is made for the Vikings. According to carbon dating of tools and utensils, vestiges of houses and workshops and even an iron foundry dug up at L'Anse aux Meadows on the northern tip of Newfoundland, suggests they sailed to the coast from Greenland around the year 1000.

This takes some of the wind out of the sails of John Cabot, the Genoese navigator who claimed Canada's eastern seaboard for his backer, the English king, Henry VII, in 1497. Local people still fight over whether it was Nova Scotia or Newfoundland he actually discovered. Cabot himself mistook it for the northeast coast of Asia. In fact, Breton, Basque and Portuguese fishermen had been here long before him but had kept the coastal waters' teeming cod fisheries secret.

Native American painting

The French came looking for gold, diamonds, spices and a passage to Asia. In 1535 Jacques Cartier ventured up the St Lawrence as far as Hochelaga Village, dominated by a hill he named Mont-Réal. Cartier was not exactly showered with honours when he returned with 11 barrels of worthless yellow iron pyrites and glittering quartz. For the next 70 years, Canada was all but ignored, until the French turned to the more lucrative new fur trade.

The strange European comings and goings were observed by Canada's native peoples whose ancestors had preceded these 'discoverers' by at least 12,000 years – some of them by 20,000 years. Waves of Siberian hunters had crossed a land bridge over the Bering Strait in pursuit of mammoths and bison. They spread through Alaska, south along the Pacific coast to the region of British Columbia, and later east across the Yukon and Northwest Territories.

Totem poles, Vancouver

New France

With no written culture to document it, the pre-European history of Canada's aboriginal peoples is a vague archaeological patchwork of bones, stones and artefacts. Their brief encounters with Atlantic fishermen left little impact, but the advent of French, and later British, colonisers brought copper kettles and guns, blankets and brandy, Christianity, measles and smallpox in exchange for their beaver pelts.

After a winter on the Bay of Fundy proved too harsh for them, Samuel de Champlain and his first batch of French settlers left Nova Scotia and moved over to the St Lawrence River in 1608. Within 10 years, both tenant farmers *(habitants)* and fur traders (*coureurs de bois*, literally wood-runners) were colonising Québec – which was known as New France – at the point where the river narrows.

To guarantee each *habitant* equal access to the waterfront, the farmland was divided into long, narrow strips reaching down to

The Early Peoples

Most Canadians have preferred to settle along the narrow strip on the American border and know very little of the northern wilderness. However, the rest of the country is far from empty, and has always been the land of Canada's aboriginal peoples.

The **Inuit** now number some 50,480, most of them gathered in village communities of stone houses, in Canada's newest province, Nunavut. More scattered groups in the High Arctic still prefer to live in traditional igloos. Their civilisation is characterised by the extremely harsh living conditions of the North.

The **Kwakiutl** live along British Columbia's Pacific coast and around Vancouver Island. Their relatively prosperous existence, due to an abundance of fish from the ocean and rivers, and the mild climate, is a far cry from the Inuit way of life. Thanks to the vast cedar forests surrounding them, carpentry became the most valued of Kwakiutl skills, and is spectacularly displayed in their totem poles.

The **Dene** nation numbers about 17,000 native people from 20 tribes in the Northwest Territories, in the western sub-arctic region. Concerned with environmental issues, the Dene nation became involved in a lengthy struggle against oil and natural gas companies, although these often seem to offer the only way out of poverty.

The **Blackfoot** used to be the great hunters of the Rockies' foothills and prairies. Buffalo then satisfied all their needs, for food, clothing, and shelter. After the herds were exterminated, mainly by the transcontinental railway builders and the Métis' rifles, the Canadian government signed the Blackfoot Treaty, under which the native people gave up their hunting grounds to raise cattle on reserves.

The **Mi'kmaq** were first called Souriquois by the French settlers. Some 20,000 remain, in 60 villages and reserves in the Atlantic provinces and Québec. They gradually gave up their traditional spiritual values for a European way of life. Salmon fishing is still an important factor in the community's economic development.

the riverbanks. Local conditions were exploited with traditional French ingenuity. Manure, for instance, was shipped downriver by heaping it on ice floes during the spring thaw. Tough *coureurs de bois* sought furs from the Huron in Ontario and the Algonquin in Québec, quickly learning the language and customs and even taking Indian wives.

Besides the huge, untapped fur resources of northern Québec and Ontario, the search continued for a northwest route from Europe to the Orient. In 1610, the British navigator Henry Hudson thought he had located the fabled Northwest Passage for his London backers when, rounding the northern tip of Québec and heading south, in the direction he hoped would take him to China, he found himself locked in a vast bay where he left his life and his name. Over 50 years later, the bay was explored by two enterprising Frenchmen, Pierre Esprit Radisson and Médard Chouart des Groseilliers. They were exasperated, on returning from their explorations with almost 100 canoes overflowing with furs, to have their entire cargo confiscated in Montréal because they had been trading without a licence.

The Hudson's Bay Company

This proved to be the beginning of the end for New France, as the two men switched their allegiance to the British. Radisson and Groseilliers's further explorations of the region, backed by British merchants, led to the founding of the Hudson's Bay Company (HBC) in 1670. Charles II granted this private joint-stock company control of all territories draining into Hudson Bay; they were named Rupert's Land after the king's cousin, who was also the titular head of the company.

The first British fur traders were better adapted to the wilderness and more understanding of the native people. From them they learned to make swift, light, birch-bark canoes, snowshoes and pemmican – a somewhat unappetising but nourishing mixture of buffalo fat with bits of dried meat and berries. The French, however, had offered higher-quality goods. The HBC was a penny-pinching company, and the First Nations soon spotted – and spat out – its raw London gin tinctured with iodine to imitate French brandy.

But Britain backed this vested interest with tough diplomacy and a powerful navy, while Louis XIV was too wrapped up in his European power plays to pay much attention to French Canada. Although the British made no military conquests in Canada during the War of Spanish Succession (1700–13), in the ensuing Treaty of Utrecht their negotiators forced the French to give up all of Acadia (Nova Scotia) except Cape Breton. There, the French fortress of Louisbourg, which defended the sea approaches to Québec, was seized by the British in 1744.

General Wolfe's troops attacking Québec in 1759

It was returned four years later in diplomatic negotiations, only to fall once and for all in 1758 in an assault mounted from the new British naval base of Halifax. In the final struggle for Québec, courageous French military commander, the Marquis de Montcalm, led outnumbered troops to a victory at Ticonderoga, but lost the city of Québec in 1759 to Britain's General James Wolfe on the Plains of Abraham. Both Montcalm and Wolfe were killed in the battle.

The French army burned its flags and sailed home, followed by most of the merchants and colonial leaders, leaving the settlers to fend for themselves. After 150 years of courageous struggle against the harsh wilderness, New France was abandoned, the old country displaying a cruel lack of enthusiasm for what Voltaire dismissed as *quelques arpens de neige* – 'a few acres of snow'.

General Wolfe was killed on the battlefield, after scaling the cliffs to reach it, while Montcalm died of his wounds the following day. Five days later, Québec surrendered.

The British Take Over

At first, British immigrants were not keen to settle in Canada either. Governor James Murray sympathised with the Québécois, whose bravery he admired. Although the church was now Anglican, Catholic privileges and tithes were restored. These were enshrined in the Québec Act of 1774, which also maintained French civil law alongside British criminal law and gave French Catholics seats on an appointed governmental council. American revolutionaries invaded Québec in 1775, hoping to win the support of French-Canadians, but to no avail. The British and Canadian garrison drove off the American attack and ended the threat to British control of Canada.

When American Independence was declared, some 70,000 United Empire Loyalists – New Englanders and Germans from Pennsylvania, but also some of the Iroquois Confederacy who had sided with the British, and liberated slaves – moved north to Canada. The majority spread out from Nova Scotia, around the Bay of Fundy, to the Eastern Townships in southern Québec and along the northern shores of Lake Ontario, including the Niagara peninsula.

To cope with the rival claims of Loyalists and Québécois, the Constitutional Act of 1791 divided the colony into Upper Canada (Ontario) and Lower Canada (Québec), separated by the Ottawa River. Under lieutenant governors, each province had a parliamentary system modelled on the Houses of Commons and Lords, while Lower Canada's French language and civil and religious institutions were safeguarded.

The land west of Ontario was written off as one big, empty wilderness until Alexander Mackenzie completed the first transcontinental crossing, and Simon Fraser and David Thompson mapped out the rivers and mountains of British Columbia and the Rockies. The Hudson's Bay Company fought for control of the fur trade with the North West Company, which was formed in 1783 in Montréal.

The Nor'westers, as they were known, commandeered the French system of forts, depots and canoe brigades, and intermarried with native people – producing the first French-speaking Métis (now a distinct nation of aboriginal people whose ancestors were partly Native, partly European fur traders). After years of fierce armed struggle for trading posts around Hudson Bay and Lakes Winnipeg and Superior, the Nor'westers threw in their lot with the HBC, bringing a wilder, more imaginative spirit to the staid old company.

With great pioneering skill, Upper Canada's first lieutenant gov-

Canada's pioneers continued to push west

ernor, John Simcoe, pushed new highways north from Lake Ontario and west to Hamilton. He established the provincial capital at a trading post, Toronto, in the heart of a malarial swamp, and renamed it York.

A landed gentry made up of army officers, government officials and commercial speculators ran Upper Canada, creating an hereditary aristocracy known as the Family Compact. The population rose from 14,000 in 1792 to 90,000 by 1812. French-Canadians were also multiplying, from 60,000 when New France was abandoned in 1760 to 330,000 just 50 years later.

Continued Hostilities

During the War of 1812, the United States was convinced that the British were backing Native American raids on settlements along the Canadian border. Congress called for nothing less than the conquest of Canada, but Major-General Isaac Brock's tiny Canadian force, allied with Chief Tecumseh's Shawnee Indians, routed a half-hearted American invasion along the Niagara frontier. The Americans burned and looted York, provoking a violent British reprisal raid on Washington.

Although they were greatly outnumbered, the Anglo- and French-Canadians fought side by side to victory at Châteauguay. Afterwards, however, the militia of Louis-Joseph Papineau's *Patriotes* became the backbone of growing anti-British agitation. With British immigration on the increase, Québécois autonomy was threatened by moves towards a single government for Lower and Upper Canada.

Landowners such as Papineau feared being swamped by projected improvements of the St Lawrence trade route. In the general paranoia, the *Patriotes* even accused the British of fostering Québec's 1832 cholera epidemic. Papineau asked London for guarantees of autonomy for a Lower Canada assembly dominated by French-Canadians. British rejection of this measure in 1837 led to riots between opposing *Patriotes* and British militia. After a victory at St-Denis, the French-Canadians were crushed by Governor John Colborne's troops north of Montréal. Defeat left an even more enduring bitterness than the original British conquest had engendered. Papineau fled to the United States.

In the same year, hatred of the high-handed Tory oligarchy in Upper Canada provoked a rebellion among small farmers and tradesmen beset by economic depression. Their champion, newspaper editor and first mayor of Toronto, William Lyon Mackenzie, proposed a US-style republic. Heeding his call, a few hundred irregulars gathered at Montgomery's Tavern north of Toronto. But a Tory militia put down the so-called Mackenzie Rebellion in a skirmish lasting just a few minutes.

Governor General 'Radical Jack' Durham was sent to put the house in order; he proposed a unified assembly governing Canada's domestic affairs. He scorned the Québécois for 'retaining their peculiar language and manners. They are a people with no history and no literature.' But Lower Canada's pragmatic Louis-Hippolyte Lafontaine accepted the British framework as a means of asserting the Québécois' right to equal representation. In the United Provinces of Canada, set up in 1841, he formed a delicate alliance with Toronto reformer Robert Baldwin.

Immigration increased to meet an ambitious public works programme of building canals to bypass the St Lawrence rapids and cross the Niagara peninsula, as well as of new cities, mines and roads. But the big news was railways.

The first, in 1836, was the Champlain and St Lawrence Railroad, a few miles of track between Montréal and Lake Champlain. By 1854 more than 400km (250 miles) of track, operated by the Great Western Railway Company, connected Niagara Falls, London and Windsor.

The dream of a transcontinental railway with freight revenues drew financiers to the Grand Trunk project to join up Montréal, the Great Lakes and the western hinterland. But initially they had to content themselves with luring American trade to the St Lawrence by linking eastern Canadian cities to Portland, Maine.

A richly decorated Native Indian ritual blanket

The Nation Takes Shape

Choosing a capital for the United Provinces wasn't easy. In the perennial Anglo-French conflict, bilingual Montréal was too troublesome, while English-speaking Toronto or French-speaking Québec City would favour one community at the expense of the other. Royal Engineer officers sent watercolours of likely sites for Queen Victoria's approval. The choice was Bytown, a lumber depot diplomatically situated between Upper and Lower Canada and renamed Ottawa, after the river on which it stood, which in turn was named after an Algonquin tribe.

To the east, and remote from the centres of power, the people of Newfoundland and the Maritime provinces lived in small, isolated communities with no unifying geography comparable to the Great Lakes or St Lawrence River. Newfoundland turned its back on the hostile interior to reap the harvests of the sea. Always psychologically closer to London than to Ottawa, Newfoundland did not become part of Canada until 1949. The Loyalists struggled valiantly with a region they called Nova Scarcity. The British had scattered Nova Scotia's French Acadians, some to the near-by islands of St Pierre and Miquelon (still French today), others as far as Louisiana, while a small nucleus remained in New Brunswick. The potential of Prince Edward Island's fertile soil was squandered by absentee land speculators who milked it only for the rents and left the settlers no motivation to develop it.

Even further away, the west was still administered as a separate empire by the HBC until gold, discovered in the Queen Charlotte Islands in 1852 and on the Fraser River six years later, prompted Britain to set up a new colony to control the influx of unruly American fortune hunters. The company's chief officer, James Douglas, became first governor of British Columbia. The company kept Upper Canadian farmers from migrating to the prairies by depicting a sub-Arctic wasteland, but British survey-ors found the valleys of the Saskatchewan, Assiniboine and Red rivers to be fertile and ideal for agriculture. The western trek began. The nation was taking shape.

French-Canadian daily life in the 19th century

Confederation

The British North America Act of 1867 created the Dominion of Canada. John A. Macdonald, an Ontario Tory, was the first prime minister. To resist a turbulent United States, torn by civil war, Anglo-Canadians wanted a strong central gov-

> **Rebel with a cause**
>
> After a period of exile in the US, Louis Riel returned to lead a second Métis rebellion in Saskatchewan in 1885. This one ended in his arrest, trial and execution.

ernment delegating little more than municipal affairs to the provinces. French-Canadians insisted on a federal system with stronger provincial governments to protect specific Québécois interests in property and civil rights. From then on, national unity would frequently play second fiddle to ethnic, religious and, above all, economic regional interests.

Only the promise of a transcontinental railway brought Nova Scotia immediately into the Confederation, with British Columbia joining in 1871, and Prince Edward Island in 1873. Rupert's Land was bought from the HBC in 1869, but incorporating Manitoba was not so easy. Led by Louis Riel, Métis descendants of Cree women and French fur traders waged an armed struggle for land rights on the Red River in the face of the expansion-hungry railway builders. An impassioned politician as well as a fiery military leader, Riel won local Anglo-Saxon support for his proposed Manitoba Act guaranteeing equal French and English language rights in schools and the Church. But the execution of Thomas Scott, a fiercely anti-Catholic Orangeman from Toronto, brought in a retaliatory force of Ontario troops, and Riel fled to the United States. The Métis were driven off their fertile land and back to hunting on the plains.

The Railroad Arrives

The railway created new cities like Winnipeg and Vancouver, which was the western terminus. In the face of tremendous difficulties, William Cornelius Van Horne, the general manager of the

Canadian Pacific Railway (CPR), built tracks around Lake Superior and west across the prairies to meet contractor Andrew Onderdonk's Chinese labourers – 15,000 were brought from China due to a labour shortage in Canada – working their way east through Kicking Horse Pass in the Rockies. The transcontinental dream became reality when the tracks were joined in 1885. This was a costly undertaking, however, not only in dollars, but also in public safety and human life. Forging a route through the Rocky Mountains, scores of labourers – many of them Chinese – died while hacking through terrain more suited to mountain goats and bighorn sheep than wooden ties and timber trestles.

Less spectacular than the completion of the CPR, but economically vital, was the first hydroelectric installation, which began functioning on Niagara Falls in 1895. A year later, gold was struck in the Klondike, opening up the Yukon to 100,000 panhandlers and camp followers, all hoping to strike it rich. The prairie provinces profited from soaring worldwide wheat exports.

The 20th Century

Presiding over this new prosperity was the country's first French-Canadian Prime Minister, Wilfrid Laurier, an elegant, eloquent Liberal. Completely bilingual, he was determined to forge Anglo- and French-Canadians into one nation. Visiting London for Queen Victoria's Diamond Jubilee, he charmed his hosts by declaring: 'I am British to the core.' He was knighted on the spot. But Laurier saw the limits of British support when the British and American negotiators of the Alaska boundary accepted United States claims to a southern coastal 'panhandle', which denied Canada sea access to the Yukon gold fields. He asserted greater national autonomy by taking over British military installations

Perilous passes

Gold prospectors approached the Yukon from Alaska via two dangerous mountain passes: Dead Horse Trail or the Chilkoot Trail, an old Native American route.

and shipyards at Esquimalt on Vancouver Island and Halifax, Nova Scotia. When Alberta and Saskatchewan acceded to provincial status in 1905, and the country's mining, lumber, paper and pulp industries burgeoned, Laurier championed a new transcontinental railway that would take a more northerly route to serve them – the state-owned Canadian National Railway (CNR).

Blondin crossing Niagara Falls on a tightrope in 1859

Laurier's conciliatory efforts did not diminish differences between Anglo- and French-Canadian interests. Conflicts raged over the denial of equal rights to Catholic schools in Manitoba, and a Prohibition referendum (blocked only by wine-loving Québécois). Political leader Henri Bourassa and influential editor Jules-Paul Tardivel insisted on pursuing time-honoured rural traditions. 'Our mission is to possess the soil,' they said, not to pursue 'American' obsessions with industry and money. They resented the sending of Canadian troops to South Africa to support the British in the Boer War, and were no more enthusiastic about the Anglo-French alliance in World War I. Bourassa said: 'The real enemies of French-Canadians are not the Germans but English-Canadian anglicisers, the Ontario intriguers or Irish priests.'

Autonomy and Americanisation

Under Tory government, the country supported Britain by sending 500,000 men to fight in World War I, losing over 60,000 on the battlefield. Emotional European nationalism spread to Canada. Citizens of German and Austrian origin were dismissed from public service, the German language was banned in schools, and Berlin, in Ontario, was renamed Kitchener.

But the war was good for the economy, supporting arms manufacture, the railways, and especially agriculture's huge wheat exports. Trades union membership expanded from 166,000 in 1914 to 378,000 in 1919, being emphatically more radical in the west, where workers chose to assert their new organisational strength by calling for a proletarian revolution. In Vancouver and Calgary, they cheered the Bolshevik victory in Russia. The government blamed the 1919 general strike in Winnipeg on 'enemy aliens', but the leaders were in fact British immigrants.

William Lyon Mackenzie King, who became leader of the Liberal Party after Laurier's death, made Canada progressively more independent of Britain. At the Imperial Conference of 1926 he won the acknowledgement that Canada was autonomous in external affairs and thus not subject to a common, British-dominated policy for the whole Empire. This led to the 1931 Statute of Westminster, which affected the equality of Britain and the Dominions, thus securing Canada's full autonomy in home and foreign affairs. The governor general in Ottawa became the symbolic representative of the Crown rather than of the British government. But the provinces insisted that the Constitution remain with London, rather than letting Ottawa infringe on their prerogatives.

The country came under the US economic and cultural orbit more and more. The 1920s boom years saw the growth of a 'branch-plant economy', with US automobile, rubber, chemical and clothing factories springing up around Hamilton, Oshawa, Windsor and Montréal. US radio programmes, films and magazines flooded the country. With the exception of the Group of Seven *(see page 61)*, a band of mostly Ontario-based painters who sought a distinctive 'national' style, most Canadian-born actors, musicians and writers felt obliged to seek fame in New York, London or Paris.

The 1930s

Canada's Great Depression was felt first by prairie farmers, unable to get rid of their surplus from the wheat glut of 1928. The drought in 1929 did not ease matters, and 10 more years of bad harvests meant they would not recoup their losses. Other sectors of the economy – timber, fisheries, mining and construction – ground to a halt as production outstripped demand.

Trans-Canada Airlines, the forerunner of Air Canada, started up in 1937, and air travel became vital for covering the vast distances, fighting forest fires and carrying provisions and wages to remote cor-

Immigrants from Europe (1903)

ners of the far north. Involvement in World War II began with a British Commonwealth Air Training Plan, using Canada's safer skies to prepare pilots for combat. At the outbreak of war, Canada's reputation for welcoming immigrants and refugees was tarnished by the blocking of Communists and Jews from Hitler's Germany. Asked how many he would allow in, Justice Minister Ernest Lapointe said: '*None* is too many.' After 1941, citizens of Japanese origin were interned and their property confiscated.

World War II and its Aftermath

Germany's invasion of France in the spring of 1940 increased the threat to Commonwealth countries. Consequently, in June of that year, Mackenzie King introduced legislation authorising conscription and, in August, signed a joint American-Canadian

The Prairies at the time of the 1929 Wall Street Crash

defence pact with Franklin D. Roosevelt, declaring that the two countries would do whatever was necessary to protect North America. War was again good for business. Out of a population of 11,500,000, more than a million were working directly in war-allied industries, most of them in brand new factories.

Social policies made important advances during and immediately after the war. In 1944 Saskatchewan elected North America's first socialist government – the Cooperative Commonwealth Federation (CCF). The Liberal government responded by appropriating much of the CCF's reform programme, including the introduction of North America's first universal health care system.

The consumer boom accentuated dependency on America's Canada-based manufacturers of cars, radios, televisions and refrigerators. The US was also Canada's main customer for raw materials and energy in an explosion of industrial achievement. North Manitoba nickel and Labrador iron were replacing depleted resources south of the border; huge oil strikes were made near Edmonton, Alberta, in 1947; a uranium reactor started up in Ontario in 1952; and hydro-electric plants mushroomed across the country. The St Lawrence Seaway opened in 1959. Six years later, drivers could cross the entire country on the Trans-Canada Highway (including the car ferry between Nova Scotia and Newfoundland).

The national culture fared less well. A Royal Commission on the Arts and Letters was spurned by Prime Minister Louis St Laurent as a futile body for 'subsidising ballet dancers'. More cultural aid was promised than delivered, but one positive result was the foundation of the highly creative National Film Board.

Balancing domestic interests and relations with the Americans became increasingly delicate. The first prime minister from the Prairies, Saskatchewan Tory John Diefenbaker, made himself popular with the farmers by negotiating a sale of wheat surplus to China that tripled their incomes – but unpopular with his American neighbour for doing business with the 'Communist devil'. In the wake of the 1962 Cuban missile crisis with the Soviet Union, the United States wanted Diefenbaker to accept nuclear warheads on Canadian soil. President John Kennedy attacked Diefenbaker's hesitation and prevarication, and the Prime Minister was defeated at the next election.

Canada celebrated its centenary in 1967 with a World's Fair, the Montréal Expo. It was an opportunity to assert the more cre-

Dirty Depression

In the Prairies, the Depression years, following the Wall Street Crash of 1929, were popularly known as the 'Dirty Thirties'. Gales whipped away the dried-out soil, and grasshoppers, hail and unseasonal frosts did the rest, forcing the gradual conversion of farmland to cattle pasture. In Saskatchewan, nine out of 10 families were on welfare benefit, and entire trains were used to bring in emergency food and clothing from other provinces. The prairie farmers couldn't fathom what to do with the salt cod sent in from Newfoundland, so they used it to plug holes in farmhouse roofs.

ative side of the country's identity – particularly that of Québec. Throughout the 1960s, the Quiet Revolution *(la revolution tranquille)* had been brewing, as a new provincial government took over responsibilities for health and education (which had previously been run by the Church) and promoted French-speaking enterprises, all under the slogan *maître chez nous* (masters in our own house). As the Roman Catholic Church increasingly lost its influence, the Québecois culture, and particularly the French language, became a strong point of identity. The cause of Québec's separatists was further fuelled, in 1967, by De Gaulle declaiming his famous '*Vive le Québec libre!*' ('Long live free Québec!') from Montréal City Hall.

The Separatism Debate

As a progressive minister of justice, who reformed laws on homosexuality, divorce, birth control and abortion, Pierre Elliott Trudeau was sympathetic to the French-Canadians' demand to have their language placed on an equal national footing with English. But this sophisticated, bilingual Montréal lawyer opposed what he regarded as Québec's tribalistic urge to exclude all things English from its own province. Trudeau became Liberal Prime Minister in 1968; like Wilfrid Laurier before him, he was just the kind of French-Canadian that Anglo-Canadians love. The Québécois were less enthusiastic. With the introduction of the birth-control pill, the province's birthrate dropped from the highest to the lowest in the nation, causing conservatives to worry at the waning influence of the Catholic Church and the prospect that French-Canadians would drown in a sea of Anglo-Canadians. When René Lévesque's separatist Parti Québécois was defeated in the 1970 provincial elections by Robert Bourassa's Liberals, embittered militants of the Front de Libération du Québec (FLQ) turned to terrorism. In quick succession, they kidnapped British Trade Commissioner James Cross and murdered Bourassa's Minister of Labour, Pierre Laporte. The country approved Trudeau's tough reaction: invoking the War Measures Act, he sent in 10,000 troops and arrested 468 militants. The FLQ was outlawed. Despite Lévesque's victory in 1976, Québec gradually moved away from outright separatism to a militant but more limited programme, which preserved the province's specific culture by imposing the French language in schools, industry and government. Subsequently, there was a westward exodus of Québec's Anglo-Canadians, and Toronto went on to bypass Montréal in population and as the financial core of the country.

After a brief respite, Trudeau returned for what he felt was his crowning achievement, the Constitution Act of 1982, the consummation of Canada's political identity. The act transferred Canada's constitution to Ottawa by removing the old obligation to refer amendments to London, and incorporated a new Charter of Rights and Freedoms, similar to the French Declaration of the Rights of Man. Despite a referendum vote by its citizens against separatism two years earlier, defiant Québec was the only province not to sign the new constitution, feeling its cultural

René Lévesque, founder of the Parti Québécois

specificity had not been guaranteed. Tory Prime Minister Brian Mulroney won the Québécois over in 1987 with an accord recognising them as a 'distinct society'. In the 1990s, Québec remained a part of the Canadian federation by the slimmest of electoral margins. However, in 2003, Québec rebuffed the Parti Québécois government and handed a decisive majority to a new Liberal government with a more federalist vision.

The Inuit and other indigenous peoples have also negotiated concessions for their lands and resources, and in 1999, the immense Northern Territories divided in two. The eastern half, which takes in Baffin Island, the land around Hudson Bay, and most of the Arctic islands, is now called Nunavut and essentially functions as an Inuit homeland. The remaining Northwest Territories officially retain the territory's old name, although many refer to the region as the Western Arctic. The success of Nunavut has led other native groups to settle claims with the Canadian government. In 2007, the Québec government came to an agreement in principle

Lévesque–Trudeau, a Political Duel

As a symbol of conflicting political visions of Canada and Québec, the long-standing 'duel' between Pierre Elliott Trudeau and René Lévesque continued to fuel controversy long after the two men left public office. Trudeau was voted leader of the Liberal Party in 1968 and served as Canada's Prime Minister from 1968 to 1979, and again from 1980 to 1984. His energetic manner and spin-free approach immediately attracted a strong following. In favour of a multi-cultural Canada, he imposed bilingualism at federal level, but then encountered strong opposition from Lévesque, founder of the Parti Québécois and Québec's premier from 1976 to 1985. While Trudeau was a multi-culturalist, who considered the French-speaking population an important minority in Canada, Lévesque wanted sovereignty for Québec. French became the official language of Québec but in a referendum in 1995, 50.6 percent of voters said no to independence.

with the Inuit in the northern region of Nunavik, which would ultimately allow the 11,000-strong community to have its own elected assembly. However, in a referendum on the agreement, the majority of the voters rejected the proposed agreement, believing that it would not allow them enough autonomy, and that more negotiations were in order. Canada's national unity remains a dynamic 'work in progress'.

Toronto architecture

Changes at the Top

At the end of 2005, the Liberal government led by Prime Minister Paul Martin was ousted by a no confidence vote. In January 2006, the Conservative party won the general election, with party leader Stephen Harper heading a minority government. This was repeated in October 2008, when Stephen Harper was again elected with a minority government. The political scene in Ottawa changed dramatically, following the May 2011 federal election. The Conservatives – under Harper's leadership – won the majority government while the long-entrenched Liberals suffered an ignominious defeat, managing to hold onto only 34 seats. The New Democratic party surged in popularity across Canada, including in Québec – where the separatist Bloc Québécois dropped from 44 seats to just four – to become the country's official opposition party, with 102 seats.

On one hand, it appears that Canadians desire a more right wing, pro-American government. However, the resounding support for a social democratic party that is considerably left-of-centre, suggests that the country has not fallen completely for an arch conservative, market-driven cause.

Historical Landmarks

7,000–6,000BC As the Ice Age ends, aboriginal peoples settle in the central and eastern parts of the land.

10th century Vikings from Greenland land on Baffin Island.

1497 Genoese sailor Jean Cabot explores the coasts of Labrador and New-foundland, claiming the land for the English king, Henry VII (Cabot had settled in England in 1490).

1534 Jacques Cartier sails up the St Lawrence River and claims the land for the French. He reaches a hill he names Mont Réal.

Late 16th–early 17th century French fishermen begin trading furs with the native people.

1670 The British, now rivalling the French in the fur trade, found the Hudson's Bay Company (HBC).

1713 Britain takes Newfoundland, New Brunswick and Nova Scotia.

1759 The French lose Québec to Britain.

1774 Québec Act: Restores Catholic privileges; French civil law maintained alongside British criminal law; the French language is recognised and French Catholics are given seats on an appointed governmental council.

1812–14 War of 1812 between US and Britain over boundary dispute. Canadians and Natives (both American and Canadian) fight alongside British forces.

1836 The first railway tracks are laid.

1840 Union Act: Upper Canada (Ontario) and Lower Canada (Québec) are united in the Province of Canada, also known as United Canada.

1867 The British North America Act unites New Brunswick, Nova Scotia, Ontario and Québec in a British-led confederation, the Dominion of Canada. A federal system empowers the provincial governments. Rupert's Land joins in 1869, British Columbia in 1871, and Prince Edward Island two years later.

1881–5 Construction of the Trans-Continental Railway.

c.1900 The discovery of gold in Yukon and the possibility of land and wealth attract nearly 2.5 million immigrants.

1928–38 Canadians suffer during the Great Depression.

1931 Statute of Westminster: Canada becomes a sovereign state and member of the Commonwealth, with autonomous powers.

1959–65 The St Lawrence Seaway opens, followed by the Trans-Canada Highway. Period of economic growth.

1960 Under Jean Lesage's Liberal Party, Québec's Quiet Revolution begins.

1963–8 The Front for the Liberation of Quebec (FLQ) launches several terrorist attacks around Montréal.

1967 While visiting Montréal, Général de Gaulle declares: 'Long live free Québec!'

1970 The FLQ kidnaps British Trade Commissioner in Montréal, James Cross, and Labour Minister Pierre Laporte; the latter is murdered; Cross is released after his abductors are given a guarantee that they can leave for Cuba.

1976 René Lévesque's Parti Québécois wins the provincial elections. Toronto supersedes Montréal as the economic capital of the country, and the city with the largest population, following an exodus of Anglo-Canadians. Summer Olympic Games held in Montréal.

1980 Québec's provincial government holds a referendum on support for negotiations on Québec's independence; 60 percent of the voters say no.

1982 Prime Minister Trudeau introduces the Constitution Act, transferring Canada's constitution to Ottawa. Québec refuses to sign, arguing that it affects its powers.

1989 The USA, Mexico and Canada sign an agreement founding the North American Free Trade Association (NAFTA).

1995 New referendum. A slim majority (50.6 percent) says no to sovereignty for Québec. The federal government promises reforms. An amendment recognising Québec as a 'distinct society' is adopted.

1999 Part of the Northwest Territories becomes Nunavut.

2003 Toronto is badly affected by the SARS outbreak. A programme of risk management is put in place to protect travellers' health.

2005 Overthrow of the Liberal government after 12 years of rule.

2006 The Conservative Party wins the general election, with party leader Stephen Harper heading a minority government.

2010 Winter Olympics held in Vancouver.

2011 The general election in May sees the Conservatives, still led by Harper, win a majority, with the left-leaning New Democrats becoming the official opposition.

WHERE TO GO

How do you get to know a country as vast as Canada? The answer is, of course, that you can't. Very few Canadians have fully explored their territory. Planning a visit to Canada that includes more than one destination is bound to seem intimidating, as the distances are so enormous. But the journey itself becomes a large part of the adventure, as you cross the wide-open spaces separating one city from another. You'll find suggested itineraries throughout this chapter and practical travel tips on pages 230–51.

A first visit will give you a feel for a few of the regions we describe, and you can capture the essence of Canada in a judicious combination of two or three major cities and a taste of the superb outdoor life. In this guide we do not attempt an encyclopedic coverage of every area from the US border to the Arctic Circle, but we do provide a representative sample of the country's sights.

Where to Visit – and When

This guide divides the country into six regions, each with at least one major town that is accessible by air as a launch pad from which to explore the hinterland. These regions are: Ontario; Québec; Atlantic Canada (Newfoundland and Labrador, and the Maritimes); British Columbia; the Rockies and the Prairies (Alberta, Saskatchewan and Manitoba); and the North (Yukon, Northwest Territories and Nunavut).

Ideally, you should allow three to four weeks for your trip. We offer a choice of strategies: either to start in Toronto or Montréal and take in Ontario and Québec, with side trips to the Atlantic coast or even out to the west; or to start in Vancouver or Calgary and explore the Rockies and British Columbia before heading east to Ontario or Québec, seeing the Prairies on a cross-country train

A grizzly bear in the mountains around British Columbia

The CN Tower

ride. The North, on a first trip, is strictly for the adventurous.

One of the advantages of Canada's vast size is that, apart from a couple of major attractions such as Niagara Falls, it is never overcrowded. Even in high summer there is still plenty of room for everone. However, it is advisable to make advance bookings for some popular resort hotels on the Pacific coast, in the Rockies or around the Great Lakes.

The best weather is usually in July and August, although it can get very hot in Montréal, Toronto and the Prairies. Further north, mosquitoes can be a problem in summer. Connoisseurs of the forests of Québec and the Maritimes favour the spectacular autumn, from September to mid-October. While the West Coast is mild in May and June, in central and eastern Canada you'll sometimes find snow on the ground in April and a nip in the air even in June. The period from November to April is strictly for winter-sports enthusiasts, although the warm Chinook wind along the Rockies' eastern slopes provides a welcome respite for Calgarians.

ONTARIO

This residential paradise between the Great Lakes and Hudson Bay is the country's dominant province. With more than 13 million people clustered almost entirely along the southern border, **Ontario** is Canada's most populous province – and the wealthiest. It generates some 40 percent of the gross national product from manufacturing, construction, minerals, forestry and agriculture. The vitality of the province has grown with the influx of Italian, German, Portuguese, Caribbean, Indian and Pakistani immigrants, reducing the once-overwhelming British majority to about 35 percent.

Not only has Toronto supplanted Montréal as the nation's business capital, its cultural and social life has expanded rapidly. The vibrant modern metropolis has – for the most part – managed to avoid the twin hazards of inner-city blight and violence. As the national capital, Ottawa is the inevitable butt of jokes against federal government bureaucracy, but patriots revere its parliament and the superb museums preserving Canada's cultural treasures.

Ontario has the best grandstand view of the Niagara Falls, one of the world's great natural wonders – to the chagrin of many tour operators in the US. The countryside in the south of the province is a gentle green delight. Ontario is host to two long-standing theatre festivals, the Shaw Festival at Niagara-on-the-Lake and the Stratford Festival of Canada, with its emphasis on the works of Shakespeare. Treat yourself to a cruise on the Trent–Severn Waterway, try watersports on Georgian Bay, and explore the Thousand Islands or Point Pelee nature reserve.

Ontario's traditions are perpetuated in villages, forts and reconstructions. The passage of French Jesuit missionaries is evoked at Sainte Marie Among the Hurons; there is a fur-trading post at Thunder Bay; you'll find military positions at Fort George (Niagara) and Fort Henry (Kingston); and there are reconstructions of the life of the pioneers at Upper Canada Village (Morrisburg) and Black Creek (Toronto).

Looking over Lake Ontario

Toronto by night: the Financial District is on the left

Toronto

1 Ethnically diverse, **Toronto** is Canada's largest metropolitan area, with a population of 5.4 million. It is hard to believe that this gleaming citadel of big business and the good urban life was, in 1790, a malarial swamp. Muddy York once had only a single attraction: its commanding position on Lake Ontario, from which Fort York guarded the troublesome American border. Yet in 1793 York became capital of English-speaking Upper Canada.

After the great famine of 1847, 40,000 Irish people emigrated to Toronto, soon to be joined by Jews from central and eastern Europe. Today, the influence of close to 100 different ethnic groups is immeasurable; around 43 percent of the city's population belong to a visible minority. While English is the predominant language, Italian is the second most common language used at work.

Today, the mud is neatly paved over. Yonge Street, the military highway opened by John Simcoe, the city's founder, linked the original fort to Lake Simcoe in the north. Named after Sir George Young, the British secretary of war in the 1790s, it is said to be the world's longest street, extending 1,896km (1,235 miles) from Toronto north, ending at the US border in Rainy River, Ontario. As one of Toronto's main commercial streets, it divides the west and east sides of the city. Its intersection with the elegant shopping thoroughfare, Bloor Street, is one of the city's several hubs.

Following John Simcoe's military grid pattern, Toronto's main arteries run from the lakefront north (Spadina and University avenues, Bay, Yonge and Church streets) and east–west (Front, King, Queen, Dundas, College-Carlton and Bloor streets). Our sightseeing itinerary starts at the waterfront and works north through the business district to the chic shopping and museum area. An alternative, especially if you have children, is to start near Union Station, and visit the other sights to the north before returning to the recreational attractions of the waterfront.

Waterfront Area

You will be in the minority if you don't begin your waterfront tour with a trip up the 553m (1,815ft) **CN Tower** (daily 9am–11pm; www.cntower.ca). This handsome, outsize TV antenna is named after its builder, the Canadian National railway and telecommunications company, and has become the iconic symbol of Canada.

A plexiglass lift whizzes you up the outside of the tower to the four lookout levels. First is the **Outdoor Observation Deck** and inside, the famous **Glass Floor** where you can peer down to the ground, 342m (1,122ft) below. On the next level up is Horizons Café and the **Indoor Observation Deck**. At 351m (1,150ft), **360** offers fine food in a restaurant with a 360-degree view of the city; the restaurant rotates every 72 minutes. The **Sky Pod**, located at 447m (1,465ft), is one of the world's highest public observation decks. Thrill-seekers can sign on for the newly-opened EdgeWalk, a full-circle, hands-free walk 116 storeys above the ground.

From the top you can see the whole of Toronto in a huge panorama in which the glass-and-steel skyscraper canyons of the Financial District, the geometric dome and resolutely modern structures of the Ontario Place leisure centre, contrast with the old-fashioned architecture of Victorian houses. Far beyond the city, you will see the full sweep of Lake Ontario's so-called 'Golden Horseshoe'.

Half the total population of the province is concentrated in this dense urban belt that borders the lake and stretches from Oshawa in the east to Hamilton in the west, taking in Toronto. More romantically, you may catch a glimpse of Niagara Falls or even Rochester on the lake's southern American shore.

For decades the lake's waterfront was reserved exclusively for loading docks, railway depots and factories, before Torontonians decided it was time to reclaim their waterfront for a multitude of leisure activities.

B ▶ **Harbourfront** is a vibrant, ever-changing neighbourhood reclaimed from a swampy wasteland, at the foot of the CN Tower.

No Shrinking Violets

Torontonians have a sizeable quota of civic pride. The founding fathers were, in the main, a stout bunch of upstate New Yorkers who didn't like the American Revolution. In their new home, they formed a Family Compact of financiers, bankers and lawyers and followed the fiercely stringent morals of Anglican archdeacon John Strachan to earn their city the ironic name of 'Toronto the Good'. For generations, they imposed strict drinking laws, solemn observance of the Sunday Sabbath and 'proper' dress and behaviour in public.

The Family Compact is today only a dim memory among the last scions of the FOOFs (Fine Old Ontario Families). Italians, Jews, Chinese, Greeks and Indians have brought a less austere image to the city. Self-confidence has grown since Québec's separatist troubles drove Montréal's Anglo-Canadian businesses into the welcoming arms of Toronto's Bay Street financiers. Most major Canadian banks now have their head offices in Toronto – even the Bank of Montréal. In Toronto you'll find a demand for high-quality goods, good cuisine, and bright, healthy living, plus a desire to improve the city's environment.

Rundown warehouses and factories have been turned into art galleries, bars, restaurants, boutiques, a sailing school, playgrounds in the park and chic apartments.

Summers are special on Queens Bay at the **Harbourfront Centre** (Mon–Sat 10am–11pm, Sun 10am–9pm; some events are ticketed, but many are free). The former warehouse has now been con-

Harbourfront

verted into stores, restaurants and a theatre. Patios overlook the lake, where sailing boats, dinner cruises circling the Toronto Islands and the occasional tall ship grace the waterfront. World-class dance companies perform in the Fleck Dance Theatre, and in nearby York Quay Centre a dynamic range of cultural ventures take place year-round – including World Stage, a series of contemporary Canadian and international performances. The annual International Festival of Authors in October brings together world-renowned novelists, poets, biographers and playwrights for the two-week event.

Facing Harbourfront, the breezy beaches and picnic areas of the **Toronto Islands** offer an escape from the city bustle. They were part of the Scarborough Bluffs peninsula until storms and floods in the mid-19th century broke them up into islands, joined today by bridges.

Ferryboats calling at the three main islands leave from the docks behind the Westin Harbour Castle Hotel at the foot of Yonge Street. No cars are allowed, but you can hire a bicycle, in town or on **Centre Island**. The latter is the most popular with Torontonians, and its beaches are particularly crowded at weekends. Quieter **Ward's Island**, at the eastern end, is more residential; you can join local people for their daily constitutional on the boardwalk. Swimmers tend to favour the beach at **Han-lan's Point**, to the west, behind the Toronto Island Airport. Take your pick of a harbour tour in a tall ship or a fancy yacht. Jutting out from the grounds of the annual Canadian National Exhibition ('Ex' to locals) held in late August, the striking **Ontario Place** (July–Labour Day daily 10am–8pm, mid-May–June and Sept–Oct hours vary; www.ontarioplace.com) is built on three man-made islands. It combines the atmospheres of a theme park and a cultural centre.

Its most outstanding landmark is the white geodesic dome of the **Cinesphere**. On a six-storey-high circular screen, it shows superb documentary films of spectacular natural phenomena, such as volcanic eruptions or the latest in space exploration. Currently, Ontario Place hopes to develop a year-round attraction. In the meantime, the water park, with many slides and flumes, keeps energetic children entertained for hours, and the Molson Amphitheatre offers classical, jazz and rock concerts. Seating

Cinesphere complex

under the covered pavilion costs more than on the 7,000 seats on the grass. But on a warm summer evening, nothing can beat a good view of the stage with a backdrop of Toronto's glittering night sky.

For a novel dining experience, try the **Medieval Times Dinner and Tournament**, at Exhibition Place. Knights on horseback joust in an 11th-century Spanish castle while you eat.

A former railway turning shed is now home to the **Steam Whistle** brewery and pub. Besides brewing an excellent Pilsner, it offers brewery tours and is an active supporter of Toronto's arts community, hosting exhibitions for local artists and numerous arts-oriented events.

Historic **Fort York** (between Bathurst Street and Strachan Avenue; mid-May–Aug daily 10am–5pm, Sept–mid-Dec Mon–Fri 10am–4pm, Sat–Sun 10am–5pm, Jan–mid-May Mon–Fri 10am–4.30pm, Sat–Sun 10am–5pm) has a bizarre location, sandwiched between the Gardner Expressway and the railway tracks. When Lieutenant Governor Simcoe built it in 1793, it commanded a strategic position directly on the lakeshore, facing potential attack from across the American border. In the War of 1812, retreating British forces chose to destroy it rather than let it fall into American hands. It was rebuilt in 1841 and restored in 1934 as a tourist attraction, with a diorama of the Battle of York and authentically furnished 19th-century officers' quarters, log cabins and a military hospital. In summer, you can watch troops parading in the British Army's scarlet uniforms, performing bayonet drills and firing their muskets.

The Downtown Core

The essence of Toronto, old and new, is concentrated around **Union Station**. Inaugurated by the Prince of Wales in 1927, it was a final proud fanfare for the transcontinental railways on which the country's industrial prosperity was built. The station is the concrete symbol of Toronto's position as a major commercial and industrial centre, as well as being the headquarters of VIA Rail, the main Canada-wide passenger rail service. Across

The 'meeting place'

Toronto's role as a business centre did not develop overnight. Long before the arrival of the Europeans, the Hurons were trading here. In their language, *toronto* means 'meeting place'.

the street, the venerable **Fairmont Royal York** hotel, restored to its 1929 splendour, provides an elegant venue for businessmen. It is linked to the station by a large underground concourse of shops and banks.

If the station and its hotel showed where Toronto was heading, the contemporary **Metro Toronto Convention Centre** to the west proclaims the city's triumphant arrival. Its amenities include all the latest electronic technology for audiovisual and communications services, three main halls for up to 40,000 conventioneers, banquet halls, the Grand Ball Room, and sports facilities to stretch those tired executive muscles.

One block north of the Convention Centre, the transparent **Roy Thomson Hall** provides a cultural counterpoint. At night it glows to reveal the throngs of smart concert-goers attending the Toronto Symphony Orchestra. The Edwardian **Royal Alexandra Theatre** nearby puts on the latest plays from New York and London, and the occasional Canadian production. It was restored by discount retailing tycoon, Ed Mirvish, who, with his son David, renovated London's Old Vic theatre. One block west, the Mirvishes built the magnificent **Princess of Wales Theatre**, specifically designed to house major international musicals.

Near Union Station, the **Financial District** concentrated around Bay Street illustrates the town's evolution. Almost all the neoclassical limestone and marble monuments that housed the old banks and stock exchange have been replaced by glittering steel-and-glass towers and pyramids. **Royal Bank Plaza**, at the corner of Front and Bay streets, reflects the new prosperity in the gilded glass of its windows. The interior, designed by Venezuelan architect Jesús Rafael Soto, is no less opulent: in the vast atrium thousands of aluminium cylinders gleam above a dazzling play of cascades, ponds and greenery.

Toronto's other banks have also brought in talents of international renown. The German Bauhaus master Mies van der Rohe designed the five black steel towers for the **Toronto Dominion Centre**, between Wellington and King streets, a masterpiece of sober elegance.

Nearby in **Commerce Court** is an exhilarating 57-storey glass-and-stainless-steel tower by the Sino-American architect I.M. Pei, designer of the new wing of Washington's National Gallery and the Great Pyramid for the Louvre in Paris.

North of the Toronto Dominion Centre is **First Canadian Place**, Canada's tallest office building. In one tower is the Bank of Montréal, reached across a pleasant green courtyard with smart shops around the waterfall. The second tower houses the more boisterous world of the **Toronto Stock Exchange**.

Commerce Court

There are no longer floor traders to watch, but you can see the stock prices through the glass wall of the TSX Broadcast Centre. The handsome setting of sculptures, paintings and art deco design contrasts with the computer monitors giving the latest prices from markets around the world.

South of the Toronto Dominion Centre, **BCE Place**, designed by Spanish architect, Santiago Calatrava, is another visual sensation, especially its soaring, cathedral-styled galleria. In one corner, a former branch of the Bank of Montréal has been converted into

Gargoyles on the Old City Hall

E ▶ the **Hockey Hall of Fame** (hours vary; www.hhof.com) with a collection devoted to the history of Canada's national game. Here, among the trophies, masks, skates and hockey sticks, American visitors may well recall the fact that nearly all their ice hockey heroes are Canadian-born.

A bustling underground network of concourses and escalators links the major buildings of the financial district to create a whole other neighbourhood of shopping malls, cinemas and restaurants, providing warmth and shelter in the winter and air-conditioned relief in the humid summer.

East of Yonge Street, on Front Street, the **Sony Centre for the Performing Arts** is Canada's largest performing arts venue, and was the long-time home of the Canadian Opera Company and the National Ballet of Canada (until their move in 2006 to the brand-new Four Seasons Centre for the Performing Arts, *see page 54*). Ambitious plans call for it to become a high-tech, multicultural arts centre topped by a 57-storey condominium designed by Daniel Libeskind. Next door, Canadian drama, both contemporary and classical, is given pride of place at the **St Lawrence Centre for the Performing Arts**.

One block away, at Jarvis Street, the huge and partially covered **St Lawrence Market** is open from Tuesday to Saturday. On Sunday there is an antique market and plenty of buskers and wandering musicians. Nearby **St Lawrence Hall**, once host to Victorian vaudeville, including Tom Thumb and Jenny Lind, has now been beautifully restored to its original pink and green.

In a country not renowned for its ecumenical harmony, **Church Street** is home to the Anglican St James Cathedral, the United Church's Metropolitan Church and the Roman Catholic St Michael's Cathedral, each an architectural variation of the neo-Gothic style of the Victorian era.

North of Queen Street, **Nathan Phillips Square**, named after a prominent Toronto mayor, is the centre of municipal government. In summer, festivals and concerts take place around the great pool; in winter the pool becomes a skating rink and the focus for celebrations on New Year's Eve. **Old City Hall** (Mon–Fri 8.30am–4.30pm), a grand neo-Gothic stone monument (1899) with clocktower and gargoyles, has been converted into a courthouse to make way for the modern (1965) landmark of **New City Hall** (offices Mon–Fri 8.30am–4pm, rotunda 7.30am–9.30pm), designed by Finnish architect, Viljo Revell. Its two gently curving office blocks open like the shells of an oyster over a domed 'pearl' containing the council chamber. Adorning the square is Henry Moore's statue, *The Archer*.

No tour of Toronto's civic past and present is complete without a pilgrimage to **Mackenzie House** (82 Bond Street; Jan–Apr Sat–Sun noon–

Old City Hall

5pm, May–Sept Tue–Sun noon–5pm, Sept–Dec Mon–Fri noon–4pm, Sat–Sun noon–5pm; tel: 416-392 6915), home of Toronto's first and most celebrated mayor. William Lyon Mackenzie, a Dundee-born Scot, lived here after his return from exile, having led a revolt in 1837 *(see page 24)*. In the meticulously restored interior, guides in colonial dress explain the memorabilia of the fiery newspaperman, including the hand-operated flatbed printing press on which he turned out his revolutionary newspaper, *The Colonial Advocate*.

H ▶ West of Mackenzie House, at the corner of Yonge and Dundas streets, is the giant mall of the **Eaton Centre**, the first of Toronto's temples of commerce, a spectacular showcase of galleries under an arched glass roof, with fibreglass geese suspended in a refreshing décor of greenery and flowers. The centre is named after Eatons, a great Canadian department store chain. Ironically it has now become part of Sears, but the name remains.

The Eaton Centre

Located west of Nathan Phillips Square, beyond tree-lined lawns, **Osgoode Hall** is a jewel of Georgian architecture in white limestone and amber brick, and the seat, since 1832, of the Law Society of Upper Canada. Notice the beautiful, wrought-iron 'cow gates' put up at the main entrance to keep the cattle out during those early rural days.

Across the street from Osgoode Hall is the the new home of the Canadian Opera Company and the National

Ballet of Canada, **Four Seasons Centre for the Performing Arts**, . It is the first theatre of its kind in Canada to be built specifically for opera and ballet. International experts were brought in to assist with the design and equipment, including the state-of-the-art acoustics.

On the northwest corner of Queen Street and University Street is **Campbell House** (year-round Tue–Fri 9.30am–4.30pm, Sat noon–4.30pm, mid-May–end-Sept Sun noon–4pm), where guides dressed in colonial dames' costumes will show you around the home of Sir William Campbell, Chief Justice of Upper Canada in the 1820s.

Behind the Art Gallery of Ontario *(see page 60)* in Grange Park, **The Grange** is one of the oldest remaining private mansions of early Toronto. It was built in 1817 by D'Arcy Boulton, one of the city's wealthy estate owners and a member of the much-admired and much-hated Family Compact *(see page 46)*, and its grounds stretched more than 3km (2 miles) from Queen Street to Bloor Street. Now owned and run by the AGO, parts of the building are open to the general public for tours, whilst other parts are used as exhibition spaces.

Queen's Park and Yorkville

The broad and tree-lined University Avenue makes an appropriately dignified and pleasant approach to the High Victorian, pink sandstone **Legislative Assembly of Ontario** and other government offices in the middle of the oval Queen's Park. Guided tours will show you the principal halls and chambers. From the visitors' gallery, you can watch provincial parliamentary debates when in session (February to June and September to December).

West of Queen's Park is the **University of Toronto**, one of the top universities in North America, with most of its buildings in Oxbridge Romanesque and Gothic. The medical school has had a high reputation since its researchers, Frederick Banting and Charles Best, discovered insulin in 1921. The university bookshop on College Street is one of the best in town.

Queen's Park

North of Bloor Street, between Avenue Road and Yonge Street, is **Yorkville**, one of ◀ **J** Toronto's trendiest shopping areas. In a transformation as radical as that of Harbourfront, the hippy slum of the 1960s has been transformed into a chic neighbourhood of fashionable boutiques, art galleries, pavement cafés, gourmet restaurants and colourful old houses. **Hazelton Lanes** is a delightful variation on the conventional shopping mall, where the maze of walkways and staircases around sunken courtyards has been deliberately designed to make you succumb to temptation. You might be forgiven for walking straight past the unprepossessing façade of the **Metro Toronto Library** (on Yonge Street, one block north of Bloor Street), but the subtly interconnected areas of the library's interior, designed by architect Raymond Moriyama, may tempt you to abandon your holiday and take up studying again. Five floors stacked with books surround an atrium enclosing greenery, a fountain and a pool.

Not far away, northwest of Yorkville, **Casa Loma** (1 Austin Terrace; daily 9.30am–5pm) is Toronto's answer to California's Hearst Castle. The battlements and turrets fulfilled the dreams of financier Henry Pellatt. After touring the castles of Europe for ideas, he built the 98-room mansion in the early 1900s at the then-astronomical cost of $3,500,000. He chose the oak and walnut from North America, teak from Asia, and panelling, marble and glass from Europe.

With all its terraces, massive walls and echoing rooms, Casa Loma is not exactly cosy, which may explain why Pellatt installed a hidden staircase as a secret escape route from his study (now open to the public). The opulently panelled Oak Room and the stained-glass dome, marble floors and Italianate bronze doors of the Conservatory all express the financier's megalomania. It's worth taking the long tunnel from the wine cellar to the luxurious stables, where the horses were indulged with a home decorated with Spanish tiles and mahogany.

Ethnic and Cultural Diversity

Toronto's neighbourhoods reflect the city's vibrant history, from the early Anglo-Saxon, pro-monarchist immigrants to the Afro-Caribbeans, Italians, Greeks, Chinese, Portuguese, Ukrainians, Poles, Indians and Irish – among many others – who have all poured into the city, each group carving out a neighbourhood or two for its own. You'll find Greeks on the Danforth, Italians and Portuguese on College Street and St Clair Avenue, the Chinese on Dundas Street, Indians on Gerrard Street, Jamaicans on Bathurst Street, Eastern Europeans around Roncesvalles Avenue and Bloor West Village. Anyone who relishes cultural diversity will find these neighbourhoods fascinating.

Chinatown

In typical North American style, Toronto's ethnic communities tend to move around, driven by the desire to profit from growing affluence or, at the other extreme, driven out by new construction. The highrises, inflated rents and construction of parking garages behind the New City Hall forced **Chinatown** to move west. This is the largest and best-known Chinatown in Toronto, because of the number of stores and restaurants here that stay open until late at night, and because of its proximity to public transport. In recent years, the area has had an influx of other Southeast Asian nationalities, notably Thai and Vietnamese immigrants. Around Dundas and Spadina you'll also find stores selling hardware, gifts, herbal medicine and tempting pastries.

Other ethnic groups – Portuguese, Greeks, Italians, West Indians – buy and sell at nearby **Kensington Market**, west of Spadina Avenue. It has the delightful chaos of an oriental bazaar, particularly on Saturday morning. The Jewish residents who once inhabited this Kensington Market area have moved to smarter **Forest Hill**, northwest of Casa Loma. Across the Don River you'll find *souvlaki* restaurants and *bouzouki* music in **Greektown** on the Danforth, home of the first Greek immigrants and **Little India** along Gerrard. **Little Italy**, an area shared with the Portuguese, is located along College Street.

Royal Ontario Museum

Museums

Popularly known as the ROM, the **Royal Ontario Museum** (100
Queen's Park; Sat–Thur 10am–5.30pm, Fri 10am–8.30pm) recently completed a major expansion. In addition to renovating some of the original galleries, the museum commissioned Daniel Libeskind to design the Michael Lee-Chin Crystal building, which houses six new galleries within a glittering aluminium and glass structure built on to the north side of the building – a controversial design that has occupied much print and airtime in the city.

ROM is the only museum in North America to house art, science and archaeology under one roof. Its Asian collection is world-renowned – the Chinese collection is one of the finest outside of China. The **Bishop White Gallery of Chinese Temple Art** is magnificent, with three huge wall paintings (painted around AD1300) and 14 massive wooden Buddhist sculptures created between the 12th and 15th centuries. The **T.T.Tsui Galleries of Chinese Art** span more than 6,000 years of history, and a Chinese tomb complex of huge 14th- to 17th-century stone sculptures can be seen in the **Matthews Family Chinese Sculpture Court** and the **Gallery of Chinese Architecture**. One of the new galleries, the **Prince Takamado Gallery of Japan**, was created to house ROM's Japanese art, Canada's largest collection.

Across the street is the **Gardiner Museum** (Mon–Thur 10am–6pm, Fri until 9pm, Sat–Sun until 5pm). This museum is a gem, and has been through a major expansion. Over 2,800 pieces of ceramic art spanning 3,000 years are on display, including pre-Columbian earthenware figures, Italian Renaissance majolica and Dutch and English Delftware. A modern and contemporary ceramics gallery showcases the works of artists such as Picasso and Chagall. Modern works by First Nations potters and other innovative ceramic art were specially commissioned for the re-opening.

The nearby **Bata Shoe Museum** (327 Bloor Street West; Mon–Sat 10am–5pm, Thur until 8pm, Sun noon–5pm), is unexpectedly absorbing. Its collection of more than 10,000 shoes spans over 4,500 years; footwear ranges from ancient funerary sandals

The Art Gallery of Ontario

to Chinese silk shoes, haute-couture pumps and a display of celebrity shoes including Elton John's platforms.

The **Art Gallery of Ontario** (317 Dundas Street West; Tue–Sun 10am–5.30pm, Wed until 8.30pm) reopened in 2008 after a three-year, $500 million expansion project. The transformation was largely triggered by several major donations, totalling more than 10,000 new works of art. Redesigned by Frank Gehry, the gallery's viewing space has been increased by nearly 50 percent to allow space for the newly acquired artworks. The AGO's permanent collection ranges from 13th-century European paintings to contemporary Canadian art. One of the largest of the new donations is 2,000 works from **The Thomson Collection**. Its content encompasses work from 19th- to mid-20th-century Canadian artists, including Cornelius Krieghoff and the Group of Seven, as well as medieval, Renaissance and baroque art. One highlight is Rubens'masterpiece *The Massacre of the Innocents* – purchased for a record $117 million by Kenneth Thomson (Lord Thomson of Fleet), Canadian art collector extraordinaire. Another highlight is the **Henry Moore Sculpture Centre**, which houses the world's largest public collection of this British artist's work.

The entertaining **Ontario Science Centre** (770 Don Mills Road; daily 10am–5pm) is 11km (6 miles) northeast of the city centre. Dramatically perched on a hillside that plunges down to the Don River Valley, the centre's three buildings are connected by glassed-in escalators, with stunning views overlooking the wooded ravine. In the new Weston Family Innovation Centre visitors are challenged to come up with ways to address real-world problems using the interactive displays and their own ingenuity. Other things to see range from experiencing the first steps on the moon through an astronaut's eyes to challenging memory tests and wandering through a rainforest – complete with a year-round climate of 28°C (82°F) and almost 100 percent humidity.

In the village of Kleinburg, 25km (15 miles) northwest of Toronto, the **McMichael Canadian Art Collection** (daily 10am–4pm) is almost entirely dedicated to the work of the Group of Seven. These landscape artists of the first half of the 20th century sought inspiration in the Canadian landscape rather than in the derivative themes of European painting. Appropriately, the museum is situated in evergreen forest overlooking the Humber valley. The stone-and-log building is a somewhat more solid version of the log cabins built by the country's earliest settlers.

The Group of Seven

Following the powerful inspiration of Tom Thomson, who died in 1917, the painters Lawren Harris, J.E.H. MacDonald, Franklin Carmichael, Arthur Lismer, Francis Johnston, A.Y. Jackson and Frederick Varley staged their first exhibition in Toronto in 1920 under the title the Group of Seven. Their initiative corresponded closely to the quest for a national identity through which Canada sought to liberate itself from the influence of Europe and the United States. 'An art,' according to Jackson, 'must grow and flower in the land before the country will be a real home for its people.'

Rejecting Europe's refined techniques, the Seven deliberately chose a style of raw, primitive vitality to evoke their country and its tough climate. But they were not impervious to the modern trends in art from across the Atlantic. The stark colours and the treatment of forms show the influence of abstract art and Cubism. And in common with European artists of the time, they were assaulted by conservative critics. When MacDonald exhibited *The Tangled Garden*, for example, he was accused of 'throwing his paint pots in the face of the public'.

Look out, too, for the Inuit and First Nations art, in particular the work of Norval Morrisseau, an Ojibwa from northern Ontario, whose works explore traditional subjects, using a modern abstract technique.

Black Creek Pioneer Village
Some 20km (12 miles) northwest of Toronto, at Jane Street and Steeles Avenue, is **Black Creek Pioneer Village** (May–June Mon–Fri 9.30am–4pm, Sat–Sun 11am–5pm, July–Aug Mon–Fri 10am–5pm, Sat–Sun 11am–5pm, Sept–Dec Mon–Fri 9.30am–4pm, Sat–Sun 11am–4.30pm). Conservationists have recreated an early Ontario log-cabin village with an 1860s farm. Riding in horse-drawn carts, you visit villagers in period costume tilling and harvesting in the fields, sheep-shearing, grinding flour in the mill, or weaving and fashioning horseshoes in the smithy. Home-cooked meals are served at the Half Way House inn.

Niagara Peninsula
To get to Niagara Falls (130km/80 miles south of Toronto) allow a 90-minute drive that curves around the western end of Lake Ontario. You will cross the Golden Horseshoe, the industrial heartland of the province that takes in Burlington, Hamilton and St Catharines. If you want to see the falls without a crowd of visitors – about 12 million people come to see them annually – then spend the night in the quieter town of Niagara-on-the-Lake, just a half-hour's drive away, and go to see the falls at off-peak times.

Niagara Falls
The true marvel of **Niagara Falls** is how nature manages to triumph over tawdry commercialism, which is somewhat less strident on the Canadian than on the American side of the border marked by the falls. Nothing can diminish the spectacle of that mass of white water taking its awesome plunge on the way from Lake Erie towards Lake Ontario and the Atlantic.

Mere statistics – an average of 2,830 cubic m (100,000

Niagara Falls, one of Canada's natural wonders

cubic ft) of water per second generating 4 million kilowatts of energy – convey nothing of the falls' immensity. You must see them close-up. The Niagara River divides into two major cascades around Goat Island: to the east, the **American Falls** (56m/180ft high with a crestline of 328m/1,075ft) and to the west, the more dramatic Canadian **Horseshoe Falls** (52m/170ft high with a curving crestline of 675m/2,200ft), and a more modest cascade off to the side, known as the Bridal Veil.

There are several vantage points from which to view the falls. **Table Rock**, named after a ledge that has long since fallen into the river, is right on the brink of the Canadian Horseshoe Falls. Down below, the Journey Behind the Falls takes you *behind* the mighty wall of water. With the price of the ticket, you borrow some protective clothing, but nothing is totally waterproof against Niagara. Don't let that worry you, just keep a change of dry clothing in the car. A tour below the falls in one of the four boats called *Maid of the Mist* takes you past and close to the foot of both falls.

The Whirlpool Aero Car gives you a bird's-eye view of the Niagara Whirlpool rapids, 4.5km (3 miles) down-river. For a superb overall view of the site, try the Skylon and Minolta towers. The **Niagara Daredevil Exhibit** (in the IMAX Theatre, 6170 Fallsview Boulevard; daily 9am–8pm) documents the attempts of those who have tried to take on the falls, and includes a collection of the original daredevil barrels.

Away from the hustle and hype, **Queen Victoria Park** is a delight for hikers, cyclists and picnickers – even cross-country skiers in the winter months. In spring, the park gardens put on a magnificent show of daffodils, tulips, magnolias and roses, and diners in the park restaurant get a fairytale view of the falls illuminated at night.

Niagara-on-the-Lake
A meandering 30km (18-mile) riverside drive north along the lovely tree-lined Niagara Parkway takes you from the tumult

Barrelling Over

In 1859, the French tightrope walker Blondin made his way across Niagara Falls on a high wire. Subsequently, others came into closer contact with the waters by going over the Horseshoe Falls in a barrel or reinforced rubber ball. (Some of the contraptions used are on show at the Niagara Falls Museum, 5651 River Road.) Ten have taken the plunge, but only seven survived to tell the tale. The first to go over, in 1901, was a woman, Annie Taylor, who hoped to make money from the publicity. She went on tour as 'Queen of the Mist', but someone stole her barrel and she died in poverty.

Londoner Bobby Leach survived his leap with a broken jaw and kneecaps. All that was found of barber Charlie Stevens was his right arm. A Greek cook went over with his pet turtle; only the turtle survived. Daredevils should know that since 1951, following the third fatal accident, you need a Niagara Parks Commission permit to go over the falls.

of the tourist buses to the tranquillity of this Loyalist bastion. Founded by opponents of the American Revolution in 1792, **Niagara-on-the-Lake** later briefly became the capital of Upper Canada. It jealously preserves its British way of life. The main thoroughfare, Queen Street, recreates the Anglo-Saxon myth with its clock tower, white clapboard and

Peach trees on Niagara Parkway

red-brick houses, the grand Prince of Wales Hotel, tea shops serving buns and buttered scones. The **Niagara Apothecary**, a pharmacy built in 1866 and lovingly restored, displays old-fashioned medicine jars in walnut cabinets under ornamental crystal gaslights.

On the quiet avenues off the main street, you can sample something of the genteel life in delightful bed-and-breakfasts that supplement the usual hotels. They are generally open from April to November, when the town hosts its renowned and popular **Shaw Festival**. Works by George Bernard Shaw and other major playwrights are performed in the modern Festival Theatre (Wellington Street and Queen's Parade Road), set in a pleasant garden where you can enjoy a cocktail during the interval. A couple of smaller theatres put on musical comedies and light revues.

On the outskirts of town, **Fort George** (daily May–Oct 10am–5pm, Apr and Nov Sat–Sun 10am–5pm) was occupied by a British garrison on the Niagara frontier in the 1812 Anglo-American war. It was destroyed, rebuilt, and then restored in the 1940s. Its outer wall, formed from a stockade of earth-and-log bastions connected by a wooden palisade, surrounds workshops, a hospital, kitchens and the 1796 stone powder house. Infantry drills are staged in the summer.

The Niagara Peninsula is one of Canada's two key wine-growing regions (the other is the Okanagan Valley in British Columbia, *see page 180*). About 50 wineries here produce some of the country's finest wines, including its multi-award-winning ice wine. Many are open for tours all year round.

Stratford

In the heart of the peninsula, 130km (80 miles) from Toronto, **Stratford**, named in honour of Shakespeare, whose birthplace was Stratford-upon-Avon in England, is well worth a detour, if only for its celebrated **Stratford Shakespeare Festival**. Inaugurated by English director Sir Tyrone Guthrie in 1953, the festival runs from April to October, with the emphasis on Shakespeare and playwrights such as Sheridan and Marlowe. The **Festival Theatre** was opened in 1957 and its apron-stage has influenced a generation of theatre-builders. The festival now includes three other stages, the **Avon Theatre**, the **Tom Patterson Theatre** and the **Studio Theatre,** and features jazz and chamber-music concerts and the work of young Canadian playwrights. Over 500,000 people come here annually.

Every effort is made to sustain an Elizabethan atmosphere. Curtain times, for example, are heralded by trumpeters in Renaissance doublet and hose. Picnic in **Queen's Park** and feed the swans on Victoria Lake. The **Shakespeare Gardens** display flowers mentioned in the Bard's sonnets and plays.

London

All roads in southwestern Ontario eventually lead to **London**, 60km (37 miles) south of Stratford. Yet, by failing to become the capital of Upper Canada, London remained small until it became the district seat in 1826. British tradition and the American feeling of wide open spaces are in harmony here. On the street signs of London names such as Oxford and Piccadilly mix with names from Ontario's history, including Simcoe, Talbot and Dundas Street. Other names – Wonderland Road and Storybook Gardens,

London: The Forest City

for example – may lead visitors to think that they have stumbled into a kind of Neverland – an impression reinforced by the squeaky cleanness, and greenness, of this city. It isn't called 'the forest city' for nothing; from any vantage point above the tree-tops, London visually disappears underneath a leafy blanket.

The River Thames flows through the campus of the **University of Western Ontario**, which has a strong presence in town. London is also home to the **Fanshawe Pioneer Village** (mid-May–mid-Oct Tue–Sun 10am–4.30pm), a reconstruction of a pre-railway, 19th-century town, with log cabins, a general store, a weaver's shop and a carriage-maker's quarters. Another reconstruction is the **Ska-Nah-Doht Iroquoian Village** (mid-May–mid-Oct daily 9am–4.30pm, mid-Oct–mid-May Mon–Fri 9am–4.30pm, weekends by appointment; tel: 519-264 1562), 32km (20 miles) southwest. The settlers in this area refused to become involved in the Huron–Iroquois wars and hence became known as the Neutrals. Today, visitors can explore the reconstructed longhouses, the sweat lodge and council chambers.

Point Pelee National Park

4 Situated at the southern end of the peninsula, **Point Pelee National Park**, on the southernmost point of the Canadian mainland, is one of the country's best nature reserves. On the same latitude as northern California and Rome, its temperate climate and vegetation offer an hospitable stopover point for 347 species of birds on their biannual north–south migrations. 'Bald point', as French explorers dubbed the area, is the southern half of a 20km (12-mile) sandspit jutting out into Lake Erie. Its terrain is a mixture of marshland, forest, meadows and sandy beaches.

Beginning with a lookout tower for bird-watchers, a circular boardwalk takes you out onto the marshes to observe the flight of the redwing blackbird and purple martin; bittern stay tucked away in the reeds. Look, too, for the pink-blossomed swamp rose-mallow, unique to Point Pelee. Bicycle and hiking trails wind through the woods, where many of the trees are draped with hanging vines reminiscent of the American Carolinas.

Point Pelee National Park

In spring, the great sport is fishing for smelt during their spawning run. In September, just before the leaves start their autumn metamorphosis, trees go bright orange with the wings of millions of Monarch butterflies on their way to Mexico.

Lakes Huron and Superior

Ontario's weekend cottages and marinas hug the shores and islands of the upper Great Lakes, offering many lakeside resorts. Keen campers, hikers and canoeists can explore the national and provincial parks for a taste of the northern interior's wilderness.

Georgian Bay

Georgian Bay is almost a separate lake. An area that was once the domain of the Hurons, until their numbers were decimated by Iroquois warriors and European disease, is now a popular weekend and summer destination for Torontonians.

East of the town of Midland, **Sainte Marie Among the Hurons** (mid-May–mid-Oct daily 10am–5pm, late Apr–mid-May and late Oct Mon–Fri only) is a reconstruction of the Jesuit mission established in 1639. Today, besides some (real) Huron Indians, costumed students show you how the community worked, complete with priests, carpenters, gardeners and blacksmiths. Begin your visit with the half-hour documentary film, which will help you to understand the mission's dramatic fate.

The Huron were less interested in conversion to Christianity than in the goods to be gained from the fur traders who followed the priests on this first French settlement in Ontario. But dealing directly with Europeans threatened the position of the Iroquois as middlemen between the Huron (and Algonquin) and the Dutch and British traders in Albany, New York. In retaliation, the Iroquois killed thousands of Huron in all-out war, and two Jesuits, Jean de Brébeuf and Gabriel Lalemant, were tortured to death. Eventually, to halt the Iroquois advance, the French community of 300 people burned their own village and returned to Québec.

The simple little **Church of St Joseph** contains the tombs of the martyred missionaries. A museum outside the stockade shows aspects of the life of the 17th-century French-Canadians, including the artefacts and birchbark canoes of the fur traders.

The dramatic landscapes of **Georgian Bay Islands National Park**, a particular favourite of the Group of Seven (see box, page 59), now attract fishermen, divers and other water-sports enthusiasts. The bay's islands are said to number 30,000, if you include all the rocky outcrops and tree-clumped sandbanks, and the national park includes some of the most attractive of these islands.

Off Honey Harbour, just outside Midland, is **Beausoleil Island**, the largest of the national park's 59 islands. It offers some well-equipped campsites and is the launch pad for exploring the other islands. There are no restaurant facilities on any of the islands.

Rocks at Tobermory

Midland and Tobermory offer **boat cruises** and ferry services out to the individual islands that make up **Fathom Five National Marine Park**. These islands are renowned for their rock formations, most notably Flowerpot, where tall limestone monoliths have been eroded into bizarre vase-like shapes.

Gravenhurst, in the heart of Muskoka and its 1,500-plus lakes, is home to the **Muskoka Boat and Heritage Centre** (June–Oct Tue–Fri 9am–6pm, Sat 9am–4pm, Sun–Mon 10am–4pm, Nov–May Tue–Sat 10am–4pm), which celebrates the region's ties to boating. Located in the Muskoka Wharf, the centre showcases life aboard a section of a 'living' steamship, complete with interactive exhibits, working engine and steam whistles. You can watch boat restoration and see up to 20 classic Muskoka wooden boats.

Thunder Bay

Located on Lake Superior's northwest shore, **Thunder Bay** is an ideal springboard to the provincial and national parks of Ontario's interior. It is also worth taking a look first at the impressive **port** facilities of this western terminus of the St Lawrence–Great Lakes Seaway, which has given Thunder Bay its second name: the Lakehead. Freighters come 3,200km (1,988 miles) inland from the Atlantic to take on grain shipments from the Prairies or bring other heavy cargo to all points west in both Canada and the US. A harbour cruise starting out from the Marina Park takes you around the gigantic, fortress-like grain silos for a close-up view of the ships in dock.

Twenty minutes west of the city by car, on the banks of the Kaministikwia River, **Old Fort William** is the handsomely reconstructed former trading post of the Nor'westers (short for North West Company), intrepid rivals of the Hudson's Bay Company in the fur industry *(see page 22)*. Sheep graze on the courtyard lawns, bread is still made in the bakery, and the refectory serves hearty country fare. In the company store you can see the kind of simple copper and pewter utensils and steel knives that were more precious than gold to the Midéwiwin Indians bringing in their beaver pelts.

Kakabeka Falls

Some 40km (25 miles) northwest of Thunder Bay, in the provincial park that bears their name, the **Kakabeka Falls** are vaguely reminiscent of those at Niagara, although they enjoy a quiet natural setting. A boardwalk takes you through the woods along the Kaministikwia River to a bridge that allows you to view the falls from both sides. The 40m (154ft) cascade flows at its fullest in spring and autumn. There are good facilities here for both camping and bathing.

Quetico Provincial Park

Canoeists and hikers really intent on getting away from civilisation head two hours west of Thunder Bay along Highway 11 to **Quetico Provincial Park**. This is the country through which the Nor'westers' *(see page 71)* paddled to the remote camps of the Ojibway trappers, from whom they adopted techniques for surviving in the wilderness, such as using snowshoes, toboggans and birchbark canoes. The indigenous peoples have been here for 9,000 years. Some of them have etched in the granite cliffs their coloured pictographs of moose, caribou, bears and turtles.

Capital Assets?

Ottawa began life in the early 19th century as a lumber depot at the confluence of the Gatineau, Rideau and Ottawa Rivers – very useful log-movers, with the Rideau waterfall providing hydraulic power for the sawmills. Lieutenant-Colonel John By made it his headquarters, Bytown, for constructing the Rideau Canal as a new strategic link between Montréal and Upper Canada. There, ethnic and religious rivalries regularly exploded into riots.

In 1843, after a visit of the governor general, Protestant Orangemen left a symbolic arch of orange tiger lilies; the Catholics tore it down rather than pass under on their way to Sunday Mass. The ensuing riot left one dead and 50 badly injured. To channel people's aggression, the authorities erected a boxing ring on Rideau Street.

Despite this, the British encouraged Queen Victoria to make Bytown the provincial capital. In place of the too-English Bytown, and avoiding anything that sounded at all French, the capital was given the neutral name of Ottawa after the river on which it stood, in turn named after a tribe of Algonquin Indians.

The only road into the park leads to the Dawson Trail Campgrounds on **French Lake**, a pleasant place for a day's picnic and swimming. For longer stays, ask the information office for maps of the park's incredible network of interlocking waterways.

Taking a stroll in Ottawa

In the former mining and logging town of Atikokan you can rent a canoe (for environmental reasons no motor launches are allowed) as well as fishing equipment, with which to catch excellent pike, bass and trout, among others.

Ottawa

Selected by Queen Victoria as her Canadian capital, **Ottawa** is not a grandly designed capital in the style of Washington or Brasilia. The picturesque Rideau Canal winds through the downtown core – populated by pleasure craft during the summer, and by skaters during the winter, when this historic navigable waterway becomes a magical 7.8km (4.8-mile) roadway of ice in the heart of Canada's capital.

In the 19th century, Bytown (renamed Ottawa in 1855) was North America's most notorious work camp, with frequent drunken brawls between the lumbermen. It was in these muddy, dangerous streets that the **Parliament Buildings** were erected between 1859 and 1865, not without a degree of consternation among the Canadians.

But Ottawa's second major source of income today is tourism, because the city is pleasant, with its pretty setting of parks and waterways, and it has some world-class museums and picturesque monuments. Its brief history as the nation's lighthouse is summed up in the imposing, solid Victorian parliamentary

The Rideau Canal, with the Parliament Buildings beyond

buildings and the resolutely modern architecture of office blocks and the **National Gallery of Canada**.

Situated on the border between Ontario and Québec, Ottawa is a bilingual city, although the majority of the French-speaking community (and many excellent restaurants) are now to be found in Gatineau, which is on the Québec side of the Ottawa River.

Except for longer excursions, leave your car in the hotel car park and walk or take the bus. The complex system of one-way streets and the added confusion of curving rivers and canals, make driving a challenging business even for local people.

Parliament Area

Like their counterpart in London, the **Parliament Buildings** (daily for tours; free but undergoing major restoration work until at least 2020) are an imposing neo-Gothic pile restored from the ruins left after a devastating fire in 1916. They dominate the Ottawa River from a bluff somewhat exaggeratedly known as Parliament Hill. As a counterpart to Westminster's Big Ben, the 92m (302ft) **Peace**

Tower, with clocks on all four sides and a 53-bell carillon, was built in front of the central building as a monument to those killed in World War I. Take the lift to the observation deck for a fine view of the city, the Gatineau Hills and the Ottawa River.

Guided tours usually take in the chambers of the Senate (in place of the UK's House of Lords) and the House of Commons. If you want to attend a debate, the visitor centre under the Peace Tower can advise you on how to get a permit. North of the central block, the handsome, pine-panelled **Library of Parliament** miraculously survived the 1916 fire. This elegant gem has been restored after a four-year project to its Victorian grandeur. Beneath the formidable Gothic rotunda, you'll see an imperial, almost goddess-like marble statue of Victoria surrounded by the early prime ministers of Canada. Some of the latter's offices have been restored in the east wing, which also survived the fire.

Evoking the ceremony at Buckingham Palace, the **Changing of the Guard** (daily July and Aug 10am) by the Governor General's Foot Guards adds a degree of pomp. On summer evenings (early July–early Sept), a 30-minute sound-and-light show illuminates the Parliament Buildings to present the history of Canada.

Sparks Street Mall, the first street in Ottawa to be paved and the country's first traffic-free pedestrian zone, is a pleasant shopping area enlivened by street musicians and clowns and bordered by some first-class modern office buildings. Pride of place goes to the elegant, 12-storey, mirror-glass **Bank of Canada** (between Kent and Bank streets) designed by Arthur Erickson. The green patina of the building's copper skeleton is a discreet homage to the copper roofs on the old Parliament Buildings. Inside is the Currency Museum *(see page 82)*.

On vast, three-sided Confederation Square, notice the

The PM's place

For Canadians, 24 Sussex Drive has exactly the same significance as 10 Downing Street has for the British. The grey stone house hidden behind greenery is the official residence of the prime minister.

National War Memorial

great granite arch of the **National War Memorial**, with statues of 22 World War I soldiers and a horse-drawn cannon. Ironically, it was dedicated by King George VI just three months before the outbreak of World War II. The square's bunker-like **National Arts Centre** (1969) is Canada's premier showcase for the performing arts – and home to the capital's symphony orchestra, French and English theatre, and dance. During the summer, Le Café's outdoor terrace overlooking the Rideau Canal is as popular as any of the performances inside.

On the square's north side, the **Fairmont Château Laurier** (1912), is a railway hotel built in the Renaissance-castle style favoured by the Canadian Pacific and Canadian National railway companies for their luxury hotels.

Local citizens boast that the **Rideau Canal**, which stretches 200km (124 miles) from the Ottawa River to Lake Ontario, is in winter 'the world's longest skating rink'. Built between 1826 and 1832, the canal has 47 locks. Its original purpose was military: the British Army wanted a second, more secure route connecting Upper and Lower Canada in the event of an American seizure of the St Lawrence River. Thousands of Irish labourers were specially brought to Canada to construct the canal, working for brutal taskmasters in a foul, mosquito-ridden wilderness. Yellow fever claimed 1,000 victims.

Nowadays, in summer, the canal offers boat cruises and canoeing, or you can explore its banks on a rented bicycle.

On the edge of the parliamentary district, across the Rideau Canal, is **ByWard Market** (one block east of Sussex Drive and north of Rideau Street). Since 1846, when nearby farmers traded their produce here, this has been the popular centre of town. Only one of the stalls dates back to 1867, but the market retains much of its 19th-century atmosphere. With its colourful stalls of fruit and vegetables, along with artsy shops, trendy restaurants and nightclubs, it's a lively spot to visit – day and night.

Sussex Drive

This is the grand drive along the Ottawa River to the town's smartest residential neighbourhood, home of ministers and of 'Embassy Row'.

The neo-Gothic **Basilica of Notre-Dame** (at the junction with Guigues Street) was born with the capital. The Catholic cathedral's steeples were built in 1858, although the church was not completed until 1890. Québec sculptors Louis Philippe Hébert, Philippe Parizeau and Flavien Rochon carved the pulpit, choir stalls, organ loft and bas-reliefs.

Turn off on St Patrick Street to drive through **Nepean Point Park** to a statue of Samuel de Champlain, founder of Québec, who looks west along the Ottawa River with his Huron Indian scout. Where the road crosses over the Rideau River and Green Island, look for Rideau Falls, pouring a double curtain of water into the Ottawa River.

The grey stone house behind the greenery at **24 Sussex Drive** is the Canadian prime minister's residence. **Rideau Hall**, just along the road (1 Sussex Drive), is the official residence

Giant spider sculpture outside the National Gallery

of the Queen's representative, the governor general. Except on official occasions, the guards in British uniforms will usually let you drive or walk in to admire the sweeping stretch of lawns and gardens – look for the governor's toboggan slide and skating rink.

The drive then circles the immaculate gardens and fine mansions of **Rockcliffe Park**. The road through the park leads to the **Rockcliffe Lookout** with its spectacular view over the Ottawa River and the mouth of the Gatineau. In the **Royal Canadian Mounted Police Barracks**, at the north end of St Laurent Boulevard, you can see some of the horses performing or training for the popular RCMP Musical Ride – the one occasion on which the 'Mounties' can still be seen mounted on horseback.

Museums

Situated on Sussex Drive opposite the Basilica of Notre-Dame, **F** ▶ the **National Gallery of Canada** (May–Sept daily 10am–5pm, Thur until 8pm, Oct–Apr Tue–Sun 10am–5pm, Thur until 8pm) is the creation of architect Moshe Safdie, also known for his Habitat homes in Montréal. It is worth spending at least half a day at the gallery, which houses the country's best European collections. The airy glass-and-steel construction brings natural daylight flooding into the spectacular Great Hall and all the galleries. The terrace of the main restaurant faces Nepean Point Park, while the windows of a less formal restaurant look out over the Ottawa River.

Among the most important works from the 14th–18th century in the **European collections** are: Simone Martini's *St Catherine of Alexandria*, Cranach's *Venus*, Hans Baldung Grien's *Eve, the Serpent and Death*, Hans Memling's *Virgin, Christ and St Anthony*, Bronzino's *Portrait of a Man*, Annibale Carracci's *Vision of St Francis*, Poussin's *Landscape with a Woman Washing Her Feet*, Rubens' *Entombment of Christ*, Rembrandt's *Heroine from the Old Testament* and Chardin's *The Governess*.

The 19th-century exhibits include works by Turner, Constable, Pissarro, Monet, Dégas and Cézanne. Klimt and James Ensor provide the transition to the 20th century, well represented by Matisse, Picasso, Braque and Francis Bacon.

In the **contemporary art** collections, American artists come to the fore, with works by Jackson Pollock, Barnett Newman, Kenneth Noland, the Pop Art of James Rosenquist, Andy Warhol and Claes Oldenburg, the Minimalist sculpture of Donald Judd and Dan Flavin, and Conceptualists such as Solo Lewitt and Joseph Kosuth. Contemporary Canadians represented include Guido Molinari, Yves Gaucher and Michael Snow.

Apart from some classics of the 19th century, evoking the life and landscapes of the early colonies, the best works in the **Canadian collections** are from Tom Thomson and the Group of Seven *(see box, page 61)*, including Thomson's *Jack Pine*, A.Y. Jackson's *Red Maple*, Lawren Harris's *North Shore, Lake Superior*, murals by Thomson, Arthur Lismer and J.E.H. MacDonald, and Emily Carr's *Indian Hut, Queen Charlotte Islands*.

Inuit art is well represented, with impressive sculptures, prints and drawings from the 1950s and 1960s. Also on show is the reconstructed Rideau Convent Chapel, a fine example of French-Canadian architecture of the 19th century.

The **photographic collection** covers the history of the art from William Henry Fox Talbot through Eugène Atget, Walker Evans and August Sander to the contemporary work of Diane Arbus and Man Ray.

G ▶ The majestic **Victoria Memorial Museum Building** at Metcalfe and McLeod streets houses the **Canadian Museum of Nature** (May–early Sept daily 9am–6pm, Thur–Fri until 8pm, Sept–Apr Tue–Sun 9am–5pm, Thur until 8pm). On show are the treasures uncovered by the Geological Survey of 1841, which went beyond geology and mineralogy to study Canada's palaeontology as well as its climate, forests and flora. In the east wing, there's the **Talisman Energy Fossil Gallery** presenting a unique look at the dramatic events that led to the extinction of dinosaurs and rise of mammals through a 50-million-year slice of time and utilising a large number of real dinosaur skeletons.

The **Canada Science and Technology Museum** (1867 St Laurent Boulevard; Sept–Apr Tue–Sun 9am–5pm, Apr–Sept daily) presents science through fun and games. There are views of the heavens through a huge refracting telescope, do-it-yourself demonstrations of balance and optics, and a plastic bubble with chicks hatching in front of your eyes. There's also a magnificent collection of antique cars and old train engines.

The **Canadian Aviation Museum** (daily Apr–Sept

The Victoria Memorial Museum Building

9am–5pm, Sept–Mar Tue–Sun 10am–5pm) at Rockcliffe Airport traces the history of aviation from the early flying machines to the fighters of two world wars. Look out for *Silver Dart*, the first plane flown in the British Empire, in 1909 and the sturdy bush planes used to cover the wilderness. More than 130 aircraft are displayed in three World War II hangars. Most of the wartime planes take to the skies again on Annual Aeronautical Day in June.

On LeBreton Flats, the

H ▶ **Canadian War Museum** (1 Vimy Place; May–June, Sept–Oct daily 9am–6pm, Thur until 8pm, July–Aug daily 9am–6pm, Thur–Fri until

Canada Science and Technology Museum

8pm, Oct–Apr Tue–Sun 9am–5pm, Thur until 9pm) offers an insightful look at Canada's military past. Dramatically located beside the Ottawa River, the museum's bold structure was designed by Raymond Moriyama – who, as a 12-year-old, was one of the more than 20,000 Japanese-Canadians interned by the federal government as 'enemy aliens'. Besides highlighting key events and defining moments in Canada's military history, human conflict is explored through personal stories, art, artefacts, photographs and interactive presentations. Memorial Hall is designed for reflection, with a single artefact: the headstone of the Unknown Soldier from World War I, which is directly illuminated by the sun each Remembrance Day, November 11, at 11am.

A 3-tonne stone 'coin' from the Caroline Islands stands outside the **Currency Museum** (245 Sparks Street; May–Oct Mon–Sat 10.30am–5pm, Sun noon–5pm, Oct–Apr Tue–Sat 10.30am–5pm, Sun 1–5pm). Inside you'll find currency used by Canada's First Nations – beads, wampum (black-and-white shells), beaver pelts and blankets – as well as coinage and paper currency from colonial to modern times.

Gatineau Park

Although in Québec, **Gatineau Park** is one of the most popular excursions from Ottawa, and only a 20-minute drive. The escarpment of 36,000 hectares (89,000 acres) of lakes and forest offers dramatic views over the plains of the Ottawa Valley. Hike or cycle the well-planned nature trails (details from the visitors' centre; daily 9am–5pm). There are five beaches and rowing boats or canoes can be hired on Philippe, La Pêche and Meech lakes. At Kingsmere, visit the estate where William Lyon Mackenzie King ended his days.

Gatineau Park

Eastern Ontario

The narrow strip of land between Ottawa and the St Lawrence River lies at the historic heart of Upper Canada. This was the home of early Loyalist settlers. Ships were built here to navigate the Great Lakes, and later it became the site for the key section of the St Lawrence Seaway, linking Montréal to Lake Ontario.

Upper Canada Village

The meticulous reconstruction of **Upper Canada Village** (daily mid-May–early Sept 9.30am–5pm, Sept–mid-Oct, Wed–Sun 9.30am–5pm), 86km (53 miles) southeast of Ottawa, is perhaps the best of the country's many historical showpieces. The homes of the region's first settlers had to be moved here, east of Morrisburg, when their original location was flooded in the digging of the St Lawrence Seaway. Climb the small **fort tower** for an overall view of the houses, reinstalled on the green banks of a canal. All are pre-1867 buildings, from the simple timbered sawmill or old schoolhouse to the sophisticated, brick-built **Crysler Hall**, in the Palladian style favoured by colonial landowners, from Ontario to Alabama.

Crysler was a farmer on whose land a crucial battle was fought in the Anglo-American War of 1812, marked by a monument beside the village. Period-costumed artisans demonstrate the crafts of bread-baking, weaving, ploughing and sowing. In the colonial setting of **Willard's Hotel**, you can enjoy a home-cooked hot meal or salad lunch.

Kingston

Located on Lake Ontario at the head of the St Lawrence River, 180km (112 miles) southwest of Ottawa, **Kingston** has a charm derived more from its universities and silvery-grey historic houses than from its federal and provincial prisons.

That said, the **Correctional Service of Canada Museum** at 555 King Street West (May–Oct Mon–Fri 9am–4pm, Sat–Sun 10am–4pm, Nov–Apr by appointment) is a guaranteed eye-opener. Leg shackles, jack o' nine tails and an ice-cold water bath are just some examples of 'restraint equipment' to keep order and discipline, used since the 1830s. Former correctional officers enthral visitors with their colourful tales. New exhibits portray life in prison today.

Originally a trading post for French and native peoples, Kingston became a shipbuilding naval base in the War of 1812. **Fort Henry** (daily mid-May–Sept 10am–5pm), now enlivened by nicely enacted parades, was built in 1832 as the main military stronghold of Upper Canada. The fort never fired a shot in anger, but rifles and cannons blast off for the Sunset Ceremony Series on Wednesday evenings in July and August.

Kingston's location made it capital of pre-Confederation Canada in the 1840s, and the sturdy, pillared **City Hall** with its lofty dome pays due homage to an illustrious past.

Cold Comfort

One of Québec's most popular songs, by the folk poet Gilles Vigneault, begins: 'My country isn't a country, it's the winter' ('Mon pays, ce n'est pas un pays, c'est l'hiver'). As is often the case with the Québécois, you can't tell whether they're complaining or boasting. Only the toughest tourists brave the long, icy Québec winter, when temperatures fall below freezing for up to six months. The first snow usually falls on Montréal in late October, and it continues until mid-April, with an occasional extra flurry in May. City life hibernates in the subterranean labyrinth of shops and restaurants beneath the downtown office buildings. Lakes and rivers turn to ice. Central heating fights off the biting winds, but people like to relax around a log fire into the night with the best beer in Canada or caribou, a potent mix that may include port, vodka, red wine, brandy and even a splash of maple syrup. However enjoyable this camaraderie may be, the spring thaw comes as an enormous relief, and when the maple tree sap rises in March or April, everyone gorges on baked beans with molasses, wieners and ham – cured in maple syrup, of course.

Thousand Islands

Kingston provides the best access to **Thousand Islands**, an archipelago of some 1,700 islands strung out along the St Lawrence River for nearly 80km (50 miles). You can go fishing or sailing, or enjoy a luxury three-day island cruise aboard the *Canadian Empress* steamboat. The island scenery of spruces and silver birches against grey-and-pink granite

Snow-covered Montréal

outcrops has long attracted the rich and famous. Millionaires made this their playground, with mansions known as 'cottages'. **Boldt Castle** on Heart Island (early-May–mid-Oct daily 10am–6pm) is an example. George Boldt, the owner of New York's Waldorf Astoria Hotel, began building it in 1898 for his wife, who died before it was finished. He abandoned his project, leaving an empty fortress, similar to those of the Rhine Valley. A rather different monument to Boldt is the Thousand Islands salad dressing that his chef concocted in honour of the region.

QUÉBEC

If only all Canadians would visit Québec, most would acknowledge that it is not only the 'original' Canada of the first European settlement, but also the province that most comprehensively encompasses within its borders the world's image of this huge country. To begin with, the province itself is huge: seven times the size of Britain or three times that of France. Forests cover two-thirds of the land: conifers in the north, and deciduous trees in the south, in particular the maple – whose leaf features on the national flag and which provides the delicious syrup – and the ash, oak and beech trees that blaze into crimson, amber and gold in autumn.

There are fewer beavers than in the great days of the fur trade, but still enough colonies to fell more than a few trees in forests throughout the province. Deer and moose abound; and further north there are herds of caribou.

Where it's not forest, city, or the farmland established by the habitants of the St Lawrence Valley and the Eastern Township Loyalists, it's water, water everywhere. The mighty St Lawrence River and Seaway link the Atlantic Ocean to the Great Lakes. Gigantic dams harness the water's hydroelectric power north on James Bay, and east on the Manicouagan River. Lakes and streams shimmer with salmon, trout, eel and pike.

Although Montréal is bilingual, Québec City, New France's old capital, and the rural villages along the St Lawrence and around the Gaspé Peninsula, are resolutely French-speaking. The Québécois can justly claim to be co-founders of the Canadian nation. Abandoned by what many called the 'damned French' (*maudits français*), they felt that they alone had earned the name of *canadiens*, and that their British conquerors usurped it. As a tribute to their own past courage, there is both pride and resentment in the Québécois motto *'Je me souviens'* ('I remember'). It was they who made the first and hardiest effort to hew a modern living out of this hard land.

Like colonials everywhere, their missionaries sometimes brought more religion, their traders more alcohol, and their soldiers more guns than the natives really needed. But the Québécois understood the importance of learning from the First Nations how to handle the country's wilderness. Several fur-trading *coureurs de bois* married native women, and today more than a few Québécois can trace their ancestry back to native peoples.

Outside Montréal, people don't necessarily speak English. Many make it a point of pride not to, until you've at least paid them the courtesy of a *'Bonjour'*. By Québec provincial law, public signs are predominantly in French, so in this guide we will often give you the English name plus the French version as it appears on maps and signposts.

Montréal

Québec's largest city, with 3.8 million inhabitants, **Montréal** is built on an island at the confluence of the Ottawa and St Lawrence rivers. Second in population now to Toronto, it remains a sprawling city of cosmopolitan neighbourhoods, each a delight to stroll around. Rather than risking traffic jams and parking problems, take a taxi, bus or the excellent Métro.

Mount Royal

For an overall view of the city, start with a bracing walk up the slopes of the lovely **Parc du Mont-Royal** (Mount Royal Park). Follow the footpath and stairs from the end of rue Peel or a shorter route from the Chemin Remembrance car park. The most pleasant way is to take a leisurely ride around the park in a horse-drawn carriage.

Known with characteristic local irony as *la montagne* (the mountain), the crest was observed by Jacques Cartier on his historic journey up the St Lawrence River in 1535, and he named it Mont Réal in homage to his king, François I.

From the massive timber and stone **Chalet de la Montagne**, or the steel cross at the summit (illuminated at night), you can look out over the St Lawrence flowing from the Lac des Deux Montagnes past the city on its northeasterly journey to the Atlantic. For practical reasons, Montréalers

An early start at Parc du Mont-Royal

consider that the river passes south of the city; the roads parallel to the river are designated 'east' or 'west' of boulevard St-Laurent. Down by the port are the low stone buildings of Old Montréal (*Vieux Montréal*). The concrete, steel and glass towers of the modern city cluster around boulevard René-Lévesque.

At its eastern extremity, Pont Jacques-Cartier links the island of Montréal to the man-made Ile Ste-Hélène, site of Expo '67, and to the south shore. Pont Victoria spans the St Lawrence to the south.

On the slopes of the smaller hill of Westmount, southwest of Mont-Royal, are the grand villas and mansions of Montréal's old Anglo-Canadian élite. To the north and west of the park are the city's ethnic minority quarters and the chic French-speaking borough of Outremont. On a clear day, visible to the northeast are the Laurentian Mountains and, to the southeast, the Green Mountains across the American border in Vermont.

Landscaped by Frederick Law Olmsted, creator of New York's Central Park, Mont-Royal is a peaceful retreat for city-dwellers, who come here to picnic in summer and toboggan in winter. You can sail model boats on the little **Lac des Castors** (Beaver Lake), or ice-skate when it's frozen over. A stroll around the lake will give you a sense of the town's ethnic diversity. On the park benches you may hear gossip not only in French and English, but Italian, Greek, Yiddish and Russian.

Vieux-Montréal

Situated between the rue St-Antoine and the port and flanked by rue McGill and rue Berri, **Vieux-Montréal** (Old Montréal) is the site of Maisonneuve's original settlement of Ville-Marie. All but a few stones of the 18th-century city ramparts have gone, but many historic houses have been restored to evoke some of the flavour of New France.

The picturesque **Place Jacques-Cartier** makes a good starting point for visiting the area. Once a fruit and vegetable market, the cobblestone square remains a favourite venue for flower vendors

Place Jacques-Cartier with Hôtel de Ville

and itinerant artists. Notice how the old stone buildings around the square are designed to withstand harsh winters, with tall, steep-sloping roofs to prevent snow and ice from accumulating.

Across rue Notre-Dame, the 19th-century **Hôtel de Ville** (City Hall) is a fine example of the French Renaissance style. It was from the balcony beneath the clock in 1967 that Général de Gaulle delivered his incendiary cry of '*Vive le Québec libre!*', warming the hearts of local separatists. The general was not intimidated by the statue of Lord Horatio Nelson watching him from the top of Place Jacques-Cartier. Montréal's oldest monument was somewhat provocatively erected in 1809, just four years after the British admiral's devastating defeat of the French at Trafalgar.

Diagonally opposite the Hôtel de Ville on rue Notre-Dame, **Château Ramezay** (June–mid-Oct daily 10am–6pm, mid-Oct–May Tue–Sun 10am–4.30pm) was home to the French governor Claude de Ramezay from 1705 to 1724.

It passed successively into the hands of the French West Indies Trading Company (to store its spices), the British, and, during

Notre-Dame-de-Bon-Secours

their brief occupation of the city in 1775, the American generals Richard Montgomery and Benedict Arnold. Benjamin Franklin stayed here during his fruitless attempt to win Québec over to the American cause.

The restored château is now a **museum** showcasing frontier life in New France: there is a grand colonial kitchen in the basement, and carved mahogany panelling imported from the French West Indies Trading Company offices. Also on show are Iroquois clothes and artefacts.

Rue Bonsecours is one of the main historic residential streets leading from rue Notre-Dame towards the Vieux-Port (Old Port). **Maison Papineau** at No. 440, is distinguished by its double row of gabled garrets in the roof and dates from 1785. It was the family home of Louis-Joseph Papineau, a controversial 19th-century politician, who was the leader of the militant *patriotes* but also a cautious protector of his seigneurial property *(see page 23)*. In 1837, during violent rioting, the house almost burned down. British troops rescued Papineau, who then fled the country and took no part in the later insurrection.

On the corner of rue St-Paul, **Maison du Calvet**, built in 1725 by a prominent Huguenot merchant, has been converted into an attractive inn with a restaurant (La Maison Pierre Calvet). As a Protestant, Pierre du Calvet was appointed by the British as justice of the peace but ended up in jail himself for selling supplies and information to the American invaders. With its broad chimney, limestone doorframes and gracefully tapered casement windows, the house is one of the most elegant examples from the French colonial era. The interior of rough-hewn floorboards and massive pinewood roof beams is decorated with original antiques.

Since 1772, the church of **Notre-Dame-de-Bon-Secours**, 400 rue Saint-Paul Est, has stood on the site of a chapel built for the colony's first schoolteacher, Marguerite Bourgeois, but destroyed by fire. She and three young women companions brought a civilising influence to the harshness of the beleaguered settlement. Acting as both teachers and nurses, they also took charge of the *filles du Roi* ('King's daughters'), in fact daughters of peasants and poor artisans, shipped over from France to marry farmers and fur traders. In the 19th century, Notre-Dame-de-Bon-Secours became known as the Sailors' Church, as shipwreck survivors brought hand-carved model ships as offerings of thanks. The models still hang from the ceiling, lit up now by tiny electric bulbs. Notice how the *trompe l'oeil* painting on the low arched ceiling gives the nave the feeling of a lofty Gothic cathedral. Climb the church tower for a view of Vieux-Montréal and the harbour.

All but one of the old warehouses along the **Vieux-Port** at the foot of place Jacques-Cartier have disappeared. Some have been converted into cafés or hotels; one pier now houses the **Centre des Sciences de Montréal**, complete with an IMAX theatre. Another hosts large festivals such as the Montréal International Reggae Festival and the Winter Fireworks Show. Walk along the port to **Pointe à Callières**, where the Ville-Marie settlers first landed. An obelisk on nearby **Place Royale** commemorates their adventure. At the Pointe is a statue in honour of John Young, who developed the port's commerce in the 19th century.

Historic quarter

Vieux-Montréal was officially classed an historic quarter in 1964. Its narrow streets are inherited from the French colonists and priests, who had plans drawn up in 1672.

Rue St-Sulpice takes you over to Place d'Armes, close to the site of the first French battles with the Iroquois. From the square you can see both the historic old town of the pioneers and the new city of commerce and industry. In the middle is a statue of Maisonneuve, brandishing the French *fleur-de-lys* flag that inspired the Québec provincial flag of today. The 19th-century neo-Gothic **Basilique Notre-Dame** (Mon–Fri 8am–4.30pm, Sat 8am–4.15pm, Sun 12.30–4pm) was designed by James O'Donell, an Irish Protestant New Yorker so inspired by his assignment that he converted to Catholicism. It once took 12 men to ring the great bell in the west tower, a task now automated. The dramatically ornate interior was the work of a Québécois, Victor Bourgeau. Our Lady of the Sacred Heart Chapel, behind the main altar, unites modern and traditional religious art in a more intimate setting for marriages and memorial services. A small **museum** displays church sculpture and painting, notably some almost surreal works by Pierre-Adolphe-Arthur Guindon, a

Do You Speak Joual?

The French of the Québécois, commonly known as *joual*, may hold some surprises, quite apart from its distinctive accent. It is a mixture of the French spoken by the 18th-century colonists, enriched by borrowings from English and American. *Joual* owes its name to the way the former working-classes pronounced the French word for horse, *cheval*.

Here are a few sources of confusion: *char* is not a tank, as in French, but an ordinary car; its fuel is not *essence*, but *gaz* (from the American gas); and *chauffer* (meaning 'to heat', in French) has nothing to do with temperature, it means to drive (from *chauffeur*). At meal times, remember that breakfast is *déjeuner*, lunch is *dîner*, and dinner is *souper*. American borrowings are typically direct, such as draught beer, which is simply *draffe*, or 'le truc', for 'truck'. Sometimes literal translations greatly amuse the French, such as *bas-culotte* for tights, or *bienvenue* ('welcome' in French), always given in perpetual reply to thanks.

Sulpician monk. Next to the church is the **Seminary of St-Sulpice**, Montréal's oldest surviving building, erected in 1685 to lead the missionary work among the Iroquois. The church also has North America's oldest public clock (1710).

Seminary of St-Sulpice

Place d'Armes is enclosed on three sides by modern buildings, including the huge post office tower. Close by is the serene neoclassical **Bank of Montréal**. Built in 1847, it is the English businessman's retort to Notre-Dame's assertion of indomitable French-Canadian values. The monumental entrance hall, all black marble and brass, sets the tone of Canada's oldest banking institution. The statue of *Patria* commemorates the fallen of World War I. Take a look, too, around the grand Exchange Room, which had its heyday when Canadian money was in the hands of august gentlemen, before they handed it over to Toronto's slick young financiers. A small banking **museum** shows the way it used to be, complete with a teller's window in the style used when the bank was founded in 1817.

Your tour of Vieux-Montréal finishes down by the St Lawrence River, at **Place d'Youville** (named after Marguerite d'Youville, founder of the Grey Nuns, a charitable order). The **Écuries d'Youville** (Youville Stables) are an enchanting collection of early 19th-century grey-stone gabled buildings, now containing restaurants and offices, overlooking a peaceful garden. The U-shaped courtyard makes a lovely setting for open-air plays and recitals in summer. The 'stables' were in fact a warehouse, which served for a while as a garage for horse-carriages.

Also in place d'Youville, is the red-brick former fire station which is now home to the **Centre d'Histoire de Montréal** (mid-

Jan–mid-Dec Tue–Sun 10am–5pm). Originally opened in 1983 and renovated in 2001, the museum attracts thousands of visitors each year. There are special as well as permanent exhibitions, and workshops for children. The permanent interactive exhibition offers an in-depth understanding of the history of the city. There are facilities for those doing research on the city (by appointment only). A panoramic view of Vieux Montréal can be had from the top of the building.

Downtown
The heart of Montréal's city centre is located between boulevard René-Lévesque and rue

Dorchester Square

Sherbrooke running parallel to the river, bounded by rues Guy and St-Denis. It is characterised by modern and postmodern skyscrapers, cultural complexes and shopping centres that are juxtaposed with old churches, museums and tempting all-night delis.

Start out from Dorchester Square, where the horse-drawn *calèches* wait. Artists and flower vendors sell their wares around Henry Moore's sculpture, *Reclining Nude*, and more austere statues of the Scottish poet Robert Burns and Canadian prime ministers Wilfrid Laurier and John MacDonald. The Sun Life skyscraper, built in 1933, is the city's oldest. Montréal's main tourist information centre is on the south side of the square, near the corner of rues Peel and Ste-Catherine at 1001 rue du square Dorchester. (A summer city information office is in Vieux-Montréal, at 174 Notre-Dame Est.)

Northeast along boulevard René-Lévesque is the Roman Catholic cathedral of Montréal, something of a visual oddity, at least for European visitors. The cathedral of **Marie-Reine-du-Monde** (Mary, Queen of the World) is a 19th-century, half-size replica of St Peter's Basilica in Rome. The nave is 109m (357ft) long, the transept is 73m (240ft) long, and the vault of the dome is 83m (272ft) high. The gilded bronze canopy over the high altar is a replica of that by Bernini in St Peter's. Unfortunately, there is nothing to match Bernini's great square to give you a proper perspective, and the church is dwarfed by the huge Fairmont Queen Elizabeth Hotel and the Sun Life skyscraper.

Place Ville-Marie (1962) is similarly dominated by the other side of the Queen Elizabeth, VIA Rail's Gare Central, and the soaring Royal Bank building. The Québec provincial tourist information office is at the northern corner of the square, near the intersection of rues Peel and Ste Catherine.

Place Ville-Marie is the starting point of Montréal's vast **underground city**. In self-defence against five or six months of ice, snow and slush, and also against the stifling summer heat, 500,000 pedestrians frequent the labyrinth of shops, cinemas, nightclubs, restaurants and cafés in this alternative city.

The interior of Marie-Reine-du-Monde cathedral

Guests at the Fairmont Queen Elizabeth Hotel can spend a whole night out on the town in winter without overcoat or galoshes, and happily return here on a swel-tering day in July. Some 33km (20 miles) of subterranean galleries (linked by Métro) stretch across the city, taking in place Ville-Marie and place Bonaventure, Les Terrasses, place des Arts and the Com-

plexe Desjardins, and even passing under the St Lawrence River to the suburb of Longueuil on the south shore.

Above ground, **rue Ste Catherine** is the city's main shopping thoroughfare, with department stores, cinemas, travel agencies, delicatessens and bars. More popular than chic, it is always lively. At the corner of University Street the Anglican cathedral of **Christ Church** (1859) is a classic example of elegant English Gothic style. Inside, be sure to admire the fine stone sculptures adorning the high altar.

In **rue Crescent**, as well as neighbouring rues Montaigne and Bishop, you'll find fashionable boutiques, bistros and restaurants. The Victorian stone terraced houses have escaped demolition. Restored and brightly painted, they now house off-beat shops, art galleries and singles bars.

These renovated buildings make an appropriate transition from rue Ste-Catherine to the elegance of **rue Sherbrooke**. With the **Musée des Beaux-Arts de Montréal** (Museum of Fine Arts; *see page 105*) near the intersection of rue Crescent, Sherbrooke is the town's main 'gallery row', with high-priced antiques, jewellery, silverware and Oriental carpet shops.

The **Ritz-Carlton Montréal**, even if you're not staying there, makes a good place to pause for a revitalising drink during your sightseeing tour.

Opposite the **McCord Museum of Canada's** social history *(see page 107)*, is **McGill University**, Montréal's principal English-speaking university. World renowned, it has seen pass through its doors such celebrities as Ernest Rutherford, the pioneering physicist, Stephen Leacock, the Canadi-

Gothic stylings
of Christ Church

Musée des Beaux-Arts de Montréal

an humorist, and, many insist, Jack the Ripper. Its **Redpath Museum** (Mon–Fri 9am–5pm, Sun noon–5pm) features fossils, minerals and zoological exhibits.

Founded in the early 19th century by a Scottish fur trader, James McGill, and especially respected for its engineering and medicine faculties, the university has a student enrolment of close to 33,000. In 1969, Québécois separatists staged violent but unsuccessful demonstrations in an attempt to have the university transformed into a French-speaking institution. (The city's other English-speaking college is Concordia, while the Université de Montréal and the Université du Québec à Montréal are both French-speaking.)

Between Maisonneuve and René-Lévesque boulevards, art and commerce come together at Place des Arts and Complexe Desjardins. **Place des Arts** is a modern cultural centre comprising a concert hall, two theatres and a recital room for chamber music. The Théatre Maisonneuve and the Companie Jean Duceppe are housed on top of one another in the step-pyramid style building, and the **Salle Wilfrid Pelletier**, with elegant sweeping curves, is the home of Montréal's orchestra. The Orchestre Symphonique de Montréal (OSM) has won world acclaim, drawing rave reviews on tours, and prizes for many of its recordings. Its home in Place des Arts also houses Montréal's modern art museum, the **Musée d'Art Contemporain** (see page 107).

The elegant tone of the whole complex is set in the foyer, decorated with Aubusson tapestries and sculptures in bronze, aluminium, mahogany and ceramics. Notice above the concert hall doors the soapstone carvings of the Inuit sculptor, Yununkpuk. With a capacity of nearly 6,000, the concert hall is also a venue for L'Opéra de Montréal and Les Grands Ballets Canadiens.

Across rue Ste-Catherine are the imposing glass portals of the dramatic multi-level shopping centre of **Complexe Desjardins**. Opened in 1976 during the grand building spree for the Montréal Olympic Games, it is a veritable shoppers' paradise.

Montréal's Neighbourhoods

Vieux-Montréal is essentially a tourist attraction because that is where you find the city's historical landmarks. The city centre is the place for business and for special nights out. But it's in the other neighbourhoods that people actually live.

It is here that you'll find in the architecture the missing links between the French-inspired homes of Vieux-Montréal and the international anonymity of the city centre's 20th-century skyscrapers. While the bourgeoisie's red-brick or stone houses are clearly inspired by Georgian and Victorian London and grander residences by the country houses and châteaux of continental Europe, the working-class terraced houses with outside iron staircases leading to upper floors (thus saving space inside) are a more characteristic Montréal feature.

Almost a neighbourhood in its own right, **boulevard St-Laurent** used to mark the 'border' between the Anglo-Canadians to the west and the French-Canadians to the east. Anglophones call it 'the Main' and French-Canadians make a rare compromise by calling it 'la Main'. The neighbourhood lines have blurred in recent years, but the Main stays appropriately neutral. You'll find a mix of Portuguese, Italian, Greek, Spanish, Polish, Jewish, Arab and Japanese speciality shops, grocery stores, delicatessens and cafés.

French-speaking students from the Université du Québec à Montréal meet in cafés, bistros and bookshops along **rue St-Denis**. Here, and around the tree-shaded **Carré St Louis**, nicely restored or equally nicely battered Victorian gingerbread mansions and iron-staircased terraced houses fight a picturesque rearguard action against the encroachment of the modern red-brick blocks of the university.

At the west end of the square, rue Prince Arthur is a pleasant tile-paved pedestrian mall of boutiques and restaurants. In the evening, this is one of the best places in town to listen to jazz and folk music.

Little Italy, one of Montréal's neighbourhoods

West of boulevard St-Laurent, squeezed by the urban redevelopment around the Complexe Guy-Favreau and Palais des Congrès, **Chinatown** huddles into a six-block area around rue de la Gauchetière. Some of its residents are descendants of the valiant labourers who helped to build the Canadian Pacific Railway.

Seek out Montréal's **Little Italy** north of Mount Royal around the **Jean Talon Market** on the place du Marché du Nord (Métro Jean-Talon). Some of the best trattorias in town are here, and they are by no means the most expensive. The lively, raucous market gives a distinctively Italian flavour to the fruit and vegetables of the Québec countryside. The Greeks, who number some 61,000, have mostly chosen the area around **avenue du Parc**, east of Outremont, for their cafés and tavernas.

With second- and third-generation prosperity, most of the Jewish residents have moved on from the **rue St-Urbain** neighbourhood made famous by the writings of Mordecai Richler (*The Apprenticeship of Duddy Kravitz*) to make way, gradually, for a Portuguese community. A nearby monument of Jewish folklore that no amount of urban upheavals can seem to budge is the ever-crowded **Schwartz's Delicatessen** (officially called Montréal Hebrew Delicatessen) located at 3895 boulevard St-Laurent. Assimilating more easily with the Anglo community – only Protestant schools accepted their children – Eastern European Jews have 'graduated' to wealthy Westmount or else emigrated, again, to Toronto. French-speaking Jews, more recent arrivals from North Africa, have mostly settled in middle-class Outremont.

On the north side of Mont-Royal, beyond the Chemin de la Côte Ste-Catherine, the handsome villas of **Outremont** make up the favoured neighbourhood of the French-Canadian bourgeoisie. Originally an Anglo stronghold, part of it is still known even among French speakers as Upper Outremont, family home of that splendidly ambiguous French-Canadian, former prime minister Pierre Elliott Trudeau. The street life in the 'lower' part of this independent township is lively, especially in **rue Bernard**, with its pavement cafés.

So where have all the Anglophones gone? The more fortunate among them have moved to **Westmount**. This bastion of the old Montréal élite of British origin became a prime target for the more violent members of the separatist *Front de libération du Québec*, who, in the 1960s, set off bombs in Westmount's mailboxes. Those not put off by this can still be seen in tweeds and cavalry twill, walking their dogs around **Summit Park**, where the Belvedere affords a fine view of the city.

Head for the tree-lined Summit Road, Summit Crescent and Summit Circle and you'll see their ivy-covered mansions and greystone turreted châteaux half-concealed behind trees and shrubbery at the top of a grassy slope. The architecture here is a wonderful compendium of French Romanesque, German Gothic and Italian Renaissance.

Westmount Square gives you a sharp jolt back into the 21st century, with the black steel-and-glass office buildings of Mies van der Rohe.

Dominating the skyline beyond Westmount, on the Côte des Neiges, **Oratoire St-Joseph** (St Joseph's Oratory) receives up to two million Catholic pilgrims each year. The enormous, 124m (408ft) high sanctuary – the dome is second in size only to that of St Peter's in Rome – was built between 1924 and 1955 in honour of St Joseph, the patron saint of workers. Today it commemorates the healing powers of Brother André, and holds 13,000 worshippers.

Oratoire St-Joseph

Montréal Tower at Parc Olympique

Born Alfred Bessette in 1845, one of a poor Québécois family of 12 children, Brother André was employed as gatekeeper at the monastic Congregation of the Holy Cross. He administered the 'oil of St Joseph' to the bodies of the sick in a small wooden chapel that he built with his own hands; it is still standing near the transept of the present oratory. More than a million of the faithful attended Brother André's funeral in 1937. His tomb is in the crypt, which is worth a look for the impressive rows of crutches donated by the miraculously healed, and the banks of devotional candles.

The best time to enjoy the oratory's interior is at one of the occasional Sunday afternoon organ recitals, when the 5,811-pipe organ thunders through the vast church.

Olympic Park

Situated east of the town centre, opposite Maisonneuve Park (Métro Pie-IX), the impressive complex of sports facilities built for the 1976 Olympic Games is an eloquent monument to the visions of grandeur that characterised the then-mayor, Jean Drapeau. After the sweeping redevelopment (some would call it sabotage) of the town centre and the ambitious construction for Expo '67 on the St Lawrence River, **Parc Olympique** (Olympic Park) was to be the apotheosis of his new Montréal. As you can see on one of the daily guided tours through Parc Olympique, the result is as grandiose in design as it has been ruinous in cost. The centrepiece is the **Olympic Stadium**, seating 55,000 spectators for major sporting events, rock concerts and other cultural gatherings.

Next to the stadium is the **Biodôme Montréal** (mid-June–early Sept daily 9am–6pm, early Sept–mid-June Tue–Sun 9am–5pm), an environmental museum that features the flora and fauna of four natural ecosystems – tropical rainforest, polar, marine and forest.

Botanical Gardens

Opposite the Parc Olympique across Sherbrooke Street are the city's **Botanical Gardens**. This delightful oasis of greenery contains some 22,000 species of flora from all over the world, lovingly tended to resist the rigours of the Québec climate. Among the highlights are magnificent orchids and cacti in the greenhouses and an exquisite arboretum of Japanese bonsai. The **Insectarium** (daily 9am–6pm) houses more than 160,000 species has recently undergone a complete facelift.

St Lawrence River

The warehouses and factories that lined the banks of the St Lawrence have been demolished and the waterfront given over to the public. **Le Vieux-Port** is now an entertainment area that offers evenings of music, dancing and beer under the stars, with the city skyline as a backdrop. The site of Expo '67, on two man-made islands in the St Lawrence – Ile le Ste-Hélène and Ile Notre-Dame – is now **Parc Jean Drapeau**. **The Biosphère** (June–Oct daily 10am–6pm, Nov–May Tue–Sun 10am–6pm) is located in Buckminster Fuller's geodesic dome which was built to house the

The Biosphère

US pavilion for Expo '67. It is now home to an environmental centre, focusing on the St Lawrence-Great Lakes eco-system. The fun and adventure of the world fair are perpetuated with outdoor concerts, exhibits and films on ecology, urban life, Canadian history, and future technologies.

In the middle of the island, the **Stewart Museum of the Fort** is in a reconstruction of the fort that the Duke of Wellington built 60 years after the capitulation of Montréal and the French army to the British in 1760 (fort and museum daily mid-May–Sept 11am–5pm, Oct–mid-May Wed–Mon 11am–5pm). The museum gives insight into early European exploration and the settlement of New France. In summer, military drills and parades staged here pay homage to both French and British (more precisely, the Scots Highlander) tradition. The fort's **Military and Maritime Museum** displays ship models, maps, navigational instruments and Canada's weapons and uniforms from the 17th century to World War II. Beyond Jacques Cartier Bridge is **La Ronde** amusement park (mid-June–Aug daily, mid-end May,

Sept and Oct weekends only), which offers all sorts of joy rides. Why not put the children on the Condor, a four-gyroscope whirligig, or Le Splash, a boat ride featuring a 15m (49ft) drop over a waterfall, while you watch from the sidelines?

A bridge (from the Ste-Hélène Métro station) leads to **Ile Notre-Dame**, site of the Canadian Grand Prix. Also here is the **Casino de Montréal** (daily 24 hours), with fine river and city views. On the island's southern tip, beyond the Pont Victoria, you can climb an observation tower for a view of the impressive **St Lambert Lock**, a key point on the great St Lawrence Seaway.

At the Cité du Havre, north of the Pont Victoria, is the controversial apartment complex of **Habitat**, designed by the architect Moshe Safdie for Expo '67. Its residents have a grandstand view of the river and its islands. At first glance, it resembles a set of building blocks thrown by a child in a tantrum, but on closer inspection you realise that it is an artful composition of 354 precast concrete boxes to create 158 homes of various sizes and combinations.

To see the river from the river, take a **harbour cruise** (depart from Quai Victoria, the most northerly pier in Vieux-Montréal, at the foot of rue Berri). For more sporting types, rafting expeditions also start out from Quai Victoria to shoot the famous **Lachine Rapids**. Alternatively, you can rent a bicycle for a pleasant ride along the **Lachine Canal**, dug in 1825 and deepened for the seaway in 1959. In winter, it makes a great open-air skating rink.

Museums

Among the most important of Montréal's many museums is its **Musée des Beaux-Arts** (Museum of Fine Arts; 1379 and 1380 rue Sherbrooke Ouest; Tue 11am–5pm, Wed–Fri 11am–9pm, Sat–Sun 10am–5pm). Founded in 1860, this is Canada's oldest museum. The edifice has a classical design and is faced in white Vermont marble. This material was used to stunning effect in the construction of the **Jean-Noël-Desmarais Pavilion**, an extension to the museum built in 1991, just opposite. The museum has a magnificent collection of works by European artists, including El Greco, Rubens, Hans Memling, Cranach and Poussin, and the British 18th-century masters Reynolds, Gainsborough and Hogarth. The moderns include Picasso and Giacometti. In 2001, the museum absorbed the fine collection of the **Musée des Arts Décoratifs**, which is devoted principally to international modern design in ceramics, glass and textiles from 1940 to the present day.

Allow plenty of time for your visit to the excellent **Canadian galleries**. In the section devoted to 19th-century art, look for the classic, if rather severe, portraits of Antoine-Sébastien Plamondon (1802–95) and the markedly gentler works of his Québécois student and rival, Théophile Hamel (1817–70).

Tom Thomson, the Group of Seven, and Emily Carr all have major works here. But of the moderns, the most significant represented is Paul-Emile Borduas (1905–60). His *Les signes s'envolent* and *L'étoile noire* are stark and disturbing abstracts by a man who began his career as a painter of church murals and stained glass. Rebelling against conservative religion, under the dual influences of Surrealism and psychoanalysis, Borduas led the school of Québec Automatistes, which is represented here with some outstanding works by Jean-Paul Riopelle, born in 1923.

Indigenous art at the McCord Museum

A few blocks to the east stands the small but tastefully designed **McCord Museum** (690 rue Sherbrooke Ouest; Tue–Fri 10am–6pm, Wed until 9pm, Sat–Sun 10am–5pm). The collection provides some fascinating insights into First Nations and Inuit life as well as into the world of the fur trader and other pioneers of the 18th and 19th centuries. Dominated by a striking totem pole from British Columbia, the exhibits include costumes, artefacts, paintings, drawings and magnificent old photographs from the William Notman archives, said to contain 45,000 prints and negatives.

The **Musée d'Art Contemporain** (Museum of Contemporary Art; 185 rue Ste-Catherine; Tue–Sun 11am–6pm, Wed until 9pm) houses a collection of works by Canadian and international artists.

Train enthusiasts should head for the southern suburb of St-Constant to visit the **Canadian Railway Museum** (122a rue St-Pierre; daily mid-May–mid-June 10am–5pm, mid-June–Aug 10am–6pm, Sept–

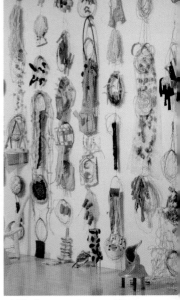

Modern art pieces at Musée d'Art Contemporain

Oct Wed–Sun 10am–5pm, Nov–mid-May Sat–Sun 10am–5pm). Visitors can ride an old tram to the country station where the sheds display historic train engines of the Canadian Pacific and the luxury private coach of William Van Horne, who masterminded the building of CPR's transcontinental railway. At weekends, you can take a ride in one of the old steam trains.

The Eastern Townships
Stretching to the border with the American states of Vermont and New Hampshire, this pleasant region of farmland and orchards was settled at the end of the 18th century by Loyalist refugees from the American Revolution. There is a distinctly New England flavour to the architecture of white clapboard

houses in a landscape of rolling hills, green meadows and lakes, but the population today is overwhelmingly French-speaking.

From Montréal taking the Autoroute 10 to the east, you can tour a sizeable chunk of the region in a day – although you may well choose to stay longer for a restful boat cruise, picnic or ramble, taking advantage of the many delightful old-fashioned country inns. The restaurants, where meals are based on the excellent local farm produce, may also tempt you.

Popular with sailing and windsurfing enthusiasts, **Lac Brome** and the sleepy town of **Knowlton** make a pleasant first stop. Continuing south to **Sutton**, you will meet farmers at the Saturday market. Long, slender **Lac Memphrémagog** (Beautiful Waters), is the region's largest lake, stretching across the border into Vermont. Boat cruises and various water sports are available at the town of Magog on its northern tip.

The church at Knowlton reflected in Lac Brome

On its west shore, look for the hillside Benedictine monastery of **St-Benoît-du-Lac** (daily 11.45am–4.30pm, July and Aug until 6pm) where you may hear the monks' Gregorian chant. The monks also make and sell fine cheeses including an Italian-style ricotta, blue Ermite and Mont St-Benoît – great with the apples from their orchard.

Further east, you'll find a strong New England atmosphere around **Lake Massawippi**, particularly in **North Hatley**, situated at the north end of the lake, where 19th-century colonial mansions have been converted into elegant inns. The town has some good antiques shops. North Hatley's location in a sheltered valley makes it the home of hummingbirds and flora normally found far to the south.

At **Coaticook**, hikers and picnickers head for the wooded ravines along the Coaticook River. In August, the town stages a milk festival with the cows (and some of the milk-maids) dressed in summer bonnets. The great attraction at

Local crafts for sale at North Hatley

Cookshire is the agricultural fair, held in August. Farther east, along with superb hiking, **Parc National du Mont-Mégantic** (Mont Megantic National Park) is hugely popular for its **Astronomy Festival** (mid-July–late Aug), held at its observatory and AstroLab.

The Laurentians

The densely forested, rolling mountain range that the Québécois call les Laurentides is a favourite, almost year-round playground for Montréalers. Swimming, sailing, canoeing, waterskiing, fishing, hiking, horse-riding, golf – the list of summer pleasures is endless. In winter, it is the best place in eastern Canada for downhill and cross-country skiing. The landscape is a pure joy, with long, narrow glacial lakes fed by cold streams gurgling down the granite mountain slopes of yellow birch, beech, sugar maple and fir. And in the autumn the leaves turn those luminous deep shades of red and orange that draw hikers, who come parading over the hills and valleys.

The virgin forests were long a refuge for Algonquin Indians fleeing the Iroquois. It was only in the second half of the 19th century that the Québécois began to settle here in any numbers when an enterprising curate, Antoine Labelle of St-Jérôme, promoted it as an alternative for peasants who were otherwise emigrating to New England. This southeastern edge of the great Canadian Shield proved poor farm country and difficult to exploit for logging, but it came into its own in the 20th century with the development of tourism. In addition to local Montréalers, it attracts steady traffic from New England.

Most of the Laurentians' resorts are within a 90-minute to two-hour drive from the city, convenient for a weekend or longer stay. Autoroute 15 northwest from Montréal, then Highway 117, take you into forested foothills just beyond the metropolis.

At only 70km (43 miles) from the city, **St-Sauveur-des-Monts** makes an excellent place to stop for lunch on one of the flowery terraced roadside restaurants. In winter, the resort is popular for floodlit night skiing. **Ste-Adèle**, on the shores of Lac Rond, is a favourite with painters and their admirers. The village of **Séraphin** has recreated the atmosphere of the 1880s.

Mont-Tremblant is the region's highest mountain at 875m (2,870ft). On the border of Parc du Mont-Tremblant, it is also one of eastern North America's top year-round travel destinations, with 95 ski and snowboarding trails. At its base, action-packed Tremblant village offers a wealth of accommodations in every price range, gourmet bistros, late-night clubs, boutiques, art galleries and festivals.

Parc du Mont-Tremblant

The full natural beauty of the Laurentians is best appreciated in **Parc du Mont-Tremblant**. Hire a canoe or kayak to explore some of the 500 lakes and rivers that sparkle across an area of 1,500 sq km (579 sq miles). It was the rush of those streams that inspired the Algonquin name Manitonga Sontana, Mountain of the Trembling Spirit. Its 1,058m (3,468ft) Johannsen peak is the

Tremblant Marina

highest in the Laurentians. At the **St-Donat** reception centre and
other entry points to the park you'll find detailed maps of nature trails with signposts describing the forest's flora and fauna.
The park also provides forest guides for group tours.

The wildlife, even more abundant in the **Rouge-Matawin Nature Reserve** to the north, includes moose, deer, bears, otters,
mink, muskrats, foxes and beavers, as well as grouse, loons,
herons, finches and warblers. Anglers can hope to catch speck-
led and lake trout, pike, bass and walleye.

Québec City

Whereas Montréal has become increasingly Americanised, the
provincial capital, **Québec City**, remains unmistakably Québécois, if not downright French. You can't help but think that, by
calling its provincial parliament the Assemblée Nationale,
Québec, the cradle of New France, is taking its cue from the modern French republic. Only about 5 percent of the population of
754,400 do not speak French.

The old town of Québec

The historic centre of the city, down by the St Lawrence River, has something of the atmosphere of French Atlantic port towns, while the streets and squares up on the promontory offer North Americans a first hint of Paris's Latin Quarter or Montmartre. Certainly it's a town for that most Parisian of creatures, the *flâneur*, or stroller, wandering at leisure through narrow back streets, paying due homage to the monuments of Québec City's past triumphs and tribulations, while all the while taking in the colours, sights and smells of the present.

The name Québec is derived from an Algonquin word meaning 'where the river narrows'; in fact the city is built on a great rock that juts out over the St Lawrence, a promontory named **Cap Diamant**, after the shiny crystals that Jacques Cartier discovered and mistook for diamonds *(see page 16)*. In the past, the city dominated river traffic and prospered from a flourishing trade in fur, lumber, shipbuilding, tanned hides, furniture and textiles. Modern shipping and the advent of the railways led to the port's decline. Today the city devotes itself to tourism, high technology and provincial government administration.

For the best view of the city's location, cross over to the St Lawrence River's south bank and take the ferry *(traversier)* from the suburb of Lévis. In any event, leave the modern city, which is agreeable but unexceptional, and of relatively little interest from a tourist point of view. Head up to **Old Québec**, which occupies

the whole of Cap Diamant. The fortified Upper Town is linked to the Lower Town by a steep road and funicular railway. Apart from the Citadel and Battlefields Park, every sight worth seeing is within easy walking distance, although you may prefer to take a 45-minute ride in a horse-drawn *calèche* from the Parc de l'Esplanade.

Upper Town

Start on top of the rock, where the city's principal landmark is a hotel, **Fairmont Château Frontenac**, which has loomed over the town since 1892 like a protective fortress it no longer needs. Its dramatic location and the fairytale turrets of its Gothic Renaissance architecture make the Frontenac one of the most ex-

Lower Town

From Dufferin Terrace, the **Basse-Ville** (Lower Town), the site of Champlain's original colony, can be reached by the winding Côte de la Montagne that skirts Montmorency Park and by various staircases of which the most perilous – and the most popular with children – is the **Escalier Casse-Cou** (Breakneck Stairway); dangerous when wet, it is lethal when icy.

For the view, take the **funicular railway** from Dufferin Terrace. The funicular's Lower Town terminal was once the house of Louis Joliet, the intrepid 17th-century fur trader and explorer of the Mississippi River.

Place Royale was the business centre of Québec City until 1832. Its name derives from the bust of Louis XIV, the Sun King of Versailles that was erected in 1686 – the bust you see today is a replica of the original. It occupies the place where, in 1608, Champlain constructed his **Habitation** – two wooden houses and a storehouse for furs surrounded by a stockade and a ditch. Today the square's elegant 17th- and 18th-century houses have been beautifully restored. The church of **Notre-Dame-des-Victoires** (daily May–Oct 9.30am–5pm, Nov–Apr 10am–4pm) dominates the square. Built in 1688, it is named for two French victories over the Anglo-Americans before 1759.

After centuries of devastation by war, fire, plunder and sheer neglect, the meticulous restoration work by the Québec provincial government has been a major act of faith in the cultural legacy of New France, reinforcing the provincial motto '*Je me souviens*'. After 1759, most colonial administrators and merchants abandoned Québec, while many who stayed on moved to the shelter of the new British defences in the Upper Town. During the 19th and early 20th centuries, older buildings were often razed arbitrarily to make way for waterfront warehouses and workshops.

Among the historic houses on rue du Marché-Champlain, **Maison Chevalier** now belongs to the Musée de la Civilisation and hosts various themed exhibitions. **Maison Lambert Du-**

mont (1689) is home to a store that sells rocks and crystals. On the corner of the ruelle du Porche, notice the sturdy roof beams of the **Maison Milot** (1691).

Several delightful **antiques shops** are clustered around rue Sault-au-Matelot and rue St-Paul, down by the port. The city has renovated the warehouses of the **Old Port** (Vieux-Port) and turned it into a new commercial and community complex with a thoroughly contemporary design. At the centre of the complex is the **Agora**, a 6,000-seat amphitheatre set attractively among flowerbeds, waterfalls and fountains and used for a variety of cultural events, particularly evening concerts in the summer.

The award-winning **Musée de la Civilisation** (daily mid-June–early Sept 9.30am–6.30pm, early Sept–mid-June Tue–Sun 10am–5pm) presents exhibitions on such subjects as language, thought, the body and society. The Vieux-Port also has a craft market, and handsome old sailing ships at anchor.

Teepee at Musée de la Civilisation

Beyond the City Wall

From the Parc de l'Esplanade, drive up the Côte de la Citadelle hill road and through a tunnel for a guided tour around what was once a powerful bastion. The French built the star-shaped **Citadel** in 1750 to resist the British. The British enlarged it in 1820 to defend Québec City against the Americans, but their cannons never fired a shot in anger. The

Festivals

Québec City thrives on festivals: early February is Carnival time, with parades and canoe-racing on the frozen St Lawrence River. In July the city streets are alive with music.

garrison was manned by the British for only 20 years before being handed over to Canadian troops. Nowadays it is the home of Canada's Royal 22nd Regiment.

In summer the garrison comes to life with the **Changing of the Guard** (24 June–first week of Sept daily 10am) and **Beating the Retreat** (July–Aug Fri–Sun 6pm). The old powder house serves now as the **Musée du Royal 22e Régiment**, retracing the history of the regiment with its trophies, weapons, uniforms and military artefacts.

Running southwest from the Parc de l'Esplanade, the broad, modern Grande-Allée passes the **Assemblée Nationale** (Provincial Parliament), built in 1877–86 in the French Renaissance style favoured at the time. It is here that Québec has fought for an identity distinct from the rest of the Canadian confederation, especially at the time of the separatist premier René Lévesque, founder of the Parti Québécois.

On boulevard St-Cyrille, the **Grand Théâtre de Québec** was inaugurated in 1971 as Québec City's arts centre and home of the Québec Symphony Orchestra. **Parc des Champs de Bataille** (Battlefields Park), at 390 rue de Bernières, is dedicated to the momentous battle on the Plains of Abraham that decided the fate of Québec in 1759. There are some delightful walks across the tree-lined fields, and is a favourite place for Québécois.

In the centre of the park is a massive **Martello tower**, constructed in 1805 as part of Québec's new defences against a potential American attack. At the end of rue Wolfe a monument marks the spot where General Wolfe was mortally wounded; anonymous Québécois patriots have 'retaliated' with a statue of Joan of Arc, off the avenue George VI.

In the southern part of the park, the **Musée National des Beaux-Arts de Québec** (June–Aug daily 10am–6pm, Wed until 9pm, Sept–May Tue–Sun 10am–5pm, Wed until 9pm) has a first-rate collection of Québécois painting and sculpture, as well as historic furniture, jewellery, and gold and silver church ornaments. The sculpture is principally from the 18th century, but the paintings range from the colony's beginnings to the present day. Look out for the historical studies of Joseph Légaré, neoclassical portraits by Antoine Plamondon and Théodore Hamel, and landscapes by Cornelius Krieghoff.

Charlevoix

A day trip along the St Lawrence River on Highway 360, north of Québec City, will give you an idea of the conditions in which the first settlers lived and the challenging landscape in which they established their farms. Renowned for its dramatic mountainous scenery, Charlevoix extends through the Laurentian shield, alongside the St Lawrence River, to the Saguenay River where the *coureurs de bois* set off in search of furs.

Sculpture at Musée National des Beaux-Arts

At the northern edge of Québec City, turn right after the Montmorency River bridge into a park where a terrace affords a fine view of the **Montmorency Falls**, plunging 91m (297ft) into the river.

Nearby is the major pilgrimage town of **Ste-Anne-de-Beaupré**. Beyond the town a walkway in the forest takes you up close to the pounding waters of the ragged

80m (262ft) **Ste-Anne Falls**, crashing around the boulders, a much less orderly cascade than Montmorency. Countless artists and artisans have chosen to live in the fishing village of **Baie-St-Paul** and its narrow streets are filled with art galleries, studios and workshops.

In a country that has one of the world's biggest paper industries, **St-Joseph-de-la-Rive** is the last town where paper is still made by hand by artisans in Papeterie Saint-Gilles. From St-Joseph, take a ferry across to **Ile aux Coudres**, another fishing community frequented by artists.

The island's crafts include weaving the rough Québécois rag rugs known as *catalognes*. You may be tempted into an overnight stay by the picturesque inns and taverns run by retired seamen, who look as if they escaped from the old schooner stranded at the southwest end of the island. They will serve you a heart-warming fish soup.

Montmorency Falls

The island owes its name to six sailors accompanying Jacques Cartier who made a feast of the island's hazelnuts, for which *coudres* is an old French word.

Since the early 20th century, **La Malbaie** has enjoyed a reputation as the region's smartest resort town, offering horse riding, golf and tennis. Even if only to have a cup of coffee, stop by at **Fairmont Le Manoir Richelieu**, an exceptional, grand old hotel with superbly manicured lawns, overlooking the river.

Gaspé Peninsula

Gaspé, where Jacques Cartier first set foot in Canada in 1534, is a Mi'kmaq Indian word for 'Land's End', and this is indeed southern Québec's most remote region, 700km (435 miles) from Québec City. But it's well worth the detour for anyone with four or five days to spare and eager to get away from the throng into this still-unspoiled wilderness on the Gulf of St Lawrence.

Route 132 loops around the **Gaspé Peninsula** in a 560km (348-mile) circle that strings together the fishing villages of the eastern coast. Densely wooded river valleys and sheltered coves break up the rugged north coast, where steep cliffs drop down to broad pebble or sand beaches. Inland, the Chic-Chocs are the highest mountains in eastern Canada: they are the northern extremity of the Appalachian Range that begins in Alabama in the US.

Although the Gaspé has been settled since the 16th century, it has suffered almost no industrial development. Even the roads and trains that came in the latter part of the 19th century left its rural tranquillity and Acadian culture largely unchanged.

The warm and friendly Gaspesians, descendants of Acadians and Loyalists, form a harmonious Anglo-French community. In a region where industry is limited to cod fishing, a little forestry and tourism, the people supplement their income by selling their craftwork and farm produce from improvised stands.

At the tip of the peninsula, **Parc National du Canada Forillon** (Forillon National Park) offers great facilities for fishing, boat cruises, diving (wetsuits are obligatory) and hiking. In the midst of these spectacular land and seascapes, even the least artistic may be tempted to take up painting, or simply to take as many photographs as possible. In the waters of the Gulf of St Lawrence, look out for humpback and minke whales, and harbour and grey seals. Wildlife inside the park includes fat little porcupine, hares, red squirrels, deer, moose and the occasional bear, lynx and fox. Birdwatchers are spoilt for choice: some 225 species live here, with guillemots and cormorants among the easier ones to spot.

To the northwest, at **Mont-St-Pierre**, near Ste-Anne-des-Monts, a hang-gliding festival is held each July, with competitors jumping over the St Lawrence.

The town of **Gaspé** makes its livelihood from fishing – cod and herring. It offers good opportunities for sailing and windsurfing (again, wetsuits are obligatory). On the rue du Monument is a **granite cross** commemorating the wooden cross that Jacques Cartier planted on behalf of his French sovereign in front of a bemused audience of Iroquois.

The best hotels are in the resort town of **Percé**, so this is naturally the most crowded place on the peninsula. People come for watersports and to marvel at the cliffs pierced *(percé)* by the sea. The most spectacular is **Percé Rock**, a 400-million-tonne block of limestone jutting improbably out of the sea. Roughly oblong in shape, it once had as many as four arches driven by the tides through the treeless crag. Try to see it at sunrise, when the sun colours the rock pink. If time permits, take a boat trip around **Bonaventure Island** to see the gannets and puffins.

ATLANTIC CANADA

The Atlantic coastal provinces lie off Canada's beaten track; this has many advantages for tourists seeking lovely, unspoilt countryside away from the crowds, but for the residents, some political and economic disadvantages. Nova Scotia, Prince Edward Island (PEI) and New Brunswick make up the Maritime provinces, more commonly known as the Maritimes. Last to join the Canadian Confederation, in 1949, the offshore island of Newfoundland is linked with the mainland region of Labrador to form a single province. These four provinces are bound together by their proximity to the Atlantic, yet each has its own cultural identity.

The Maritimes, Newfoundland and Labrador, known collectively as Atlantic Canada, have often felt neglected. They were the last provinces to benefit from transcontinental railways and highways. New Brunswick's shipbuilding timber industry suffered

Deer Island, New Brunswick

in the age of steamships and steel hulls. Newfoundland's fisheries were hard hit when refrigeration enabled foreign companies to dispense with the island's drying techniques. Economic hardship prompted some to migrate. More recently, the province's fortunes have risen again with the discovery of offshore oil.

Yet this very separateness has shaped a hardy people of considerable character and charm – qualities that make it well worthwhile getting to know them. You'll often find them cheerful, friendly and more easily approachable than the population of the big cities of Ontario and Québec.

Newfoundland is peopled almost exclusively from the southwest of England and southern Ireland, which accounts for the special music and colour of their dialect. The Maritimes have been mainly settled by Scottish Highlanders, German Protestants and French-speaking Acadians.

Because of their cool climate these regions should be visited in summer and early autumn only, when there is excellent hiking, camping and fishing, and swimming off the beaches of Prince Ed-

Setting sun on Nova Scotia's South shore

ward Island and Nova Scotia. From the end of June to the beginning of September the temperature is warm to mellow in the Maritimes but Newfoundland always tends to be a little fresher.

Nova Scotia

You might be forgiven for thinking that the chamber of commerce modified the map of Nova Scotia as a public relations gimmick. But not so: the province really is shaped like a lobster. For a number of gourmets, lobster dinner in a restaurant in Halifax is reason enough to make the trip.

The delightful fishing ports on the Atlantic coastline give way to the rolling green hills of the interior, with the orchards and dairy farms of Annapolis Valley. This western side of the peninsula is steeped in the history of French Acadia.

The province's northern island is the site of one of Canada's best-loved national parks, Cape Breton Highlands, with the spectacular Cabot Trail winding along the coast and in and out of the forest.

Halifax

Ships of the Canadian navy jostle with the trawlers of Nova Scotia's commercial fisheries in this major Atlantic port. But the prevailing tone is one of more relaxed pleasure, typified by the yachts and sailing boats gliding gracefully in and out of the Northwest Arm marinas.

Attracted by the natural harbour, in the mid-18th century the British established **Halifax** as a naval garrison and shipyard to counter the French fortress of Louisbourg further north on Cape Breton *(see page 135)*. Halifax's strategic position on the Atlantic soon proved invaluable for fishing the rich shoals of cod and herring on the ocean's Scotian Shelf. It was also a haven for pirates and rum-runners from the time of the Napoleonic Wars to the American Prohibition era of the 1920s. Samuel Cunard (1787–1865) founded his famous transatlantic shipping line with a fortune acquired in large part from privateering.

In the port today, the old wharves, warehouses and even the houses of ill-repute that flourished here have all been restored. Now named **Historic Properties**, they form a bright and breezy neighbourhood of artists' studios and galleries, shops, restaurants and taverns with open-air terraces. A boardwalk takes you through an architectural kaleidoscope of red brick, timber, grey stone and brightly painted clapboard.

The harbour in Halifax is one of the world's largest natural harbours. There are plenty of **harbour cruises** available, which are well worth taking as they offer a chance to view the shipyards, naval installations and fishing fleet, as well as the yacht clubs and elegant waterfront homes on the Northwest Arm inlet.

Also in the port, at 1675 Lower Water Street, you'll find the **Maritime Museum of the Atlantic** (May–Sept daily 9.30am–5.30pm, Tue until 8pm, Nov–Apr Tue 9.30am–8pm, Wed–Sat 9.30am–5pm, Sun 1–5pm, Oct and May Mon, Wed–Sat 9.30am–5pm, Tue until 8pm, Sun 1–5.30pm). It is housed in a restored turn-of-the-20th-century ship's chandlers, and there is still a nostalgic whiff of tarred rope. The museum traces some 200 years

Weatherboard houses in Halifax

of maritime history, displaying naval instruments, weapons and some superb models, from sailing boats to steamships, including the *Aquitania* ocean liner. A special section is devoted to ship-wrecks on the notorious Sable Island. Berthed at the museum's wharf is the 1913 survey vessel, CSS *Acadia*, on board which the measurements were taken that allowed the charting of the coasts of eastern Canada from Nova Scotia to Hudson Bay.

In the centre of town, on Hollis Street, **Province House**, a dignified Georgian stone building (1819), is home to Canada's oldest legislative assembly, instigated by New England Loyalists. A statue of Joseph Howe stands in front; he was Nova Scotia's champion of a free press and democratic government, but a fierce opponent of joining the Confederation.

For a good panoramic view of Halifax and a sense of its im-portant military history, make your way around the grassy slopes leading to the star-shaped **Citadel** (daily May–June and Sept–Oct 9am–5pm, July–Aug 9am–6pm, Nov–Apr grounds only), from which a cannon-shot has boomed across the town each day at noon since the 1850s. An excellent guided tour takes you around the garrison, originally built for 300 British soldiers. It is surrounded by a deep, wide, dry moat, thick walls and fortified, grass-covered earthworks.

The Cavalier Building has been restored to the way it was in 1869 and is now an **Army Museum** (May–June and Sept–Oct 9am–5pm, July–Aug 9am–6pm), with uniforms, weapons and the models of three previous city fortresses. The South Magazine stored powder barrels uncomfortably close to military prisoners who were kept, with the cannons, in the garrison cells. Canadian troops used the Citadel as barracks in both world wars, and anti-aircraft batteries were installed there during World War II.

In summer, students in the kilted uniform of the 78th Highlanders perform infantry and artillery drills. The **Royal Nova Scotia International Tattoo** (early July at the nearby Halifax Metro Centre) stages more spectacular military bagpipe parades, highland dances, singing, and a Naval Gun Run competition.

From the Citadel, looking east, you can see the city's popular landmark, the **Old Town Clock**. This octagonal tower was erected in 1803 by Prince Edward, Duke of Kent, the tough commander of the Nova Scotia forces (and future father of Queen Victoria), who was a stickler for punctuality. At the south end of Grand Parade, opposite the city hall, stands **St Paul's**, Canada's oldest Anglican church, which dates from 1750.

Soldiers of the 78th Highland Regiment at the Citadel

West of the Citadel, on Summer Street, is the **Nova Scotia Museum of Natural History** (June–Sept Mon–Sat 9am–5pm, Wed until 8pm, Sun 1–5pm, Oct–May Tue–Sat

9am–5pm, Wed until 8pm, Sun 1–5pm), devoted to the province's human and natural history, notably Mi'kmaq artefacts, some dating back 11,000 years. You'll see clothing, tools and artefacts, with local Mi'kmaq people demonstrating their use, and colonial ceramics, glassware and pinewood furniture, often artfully painted to imitate more expensive mahogany or oak. Regional wildlife on display ranges from moose and bears to coyotes and bald eagles. There are also excellent visiting exhibitions.

In the **Halifax Public Gardens** (daily May–Oct 8am–dusk), south of the museum, take a pleasant stroll round the duck pond and among such exotic trees as the Chinese gingko and white-flowered dove tree, the Japanese lilac and larch, and a corkscrew birch. Do your best to be here for an open-air band concert (Sundays, in summer) in the Victorian tradition. **Point Pleasant Park**, at the southern tip of the peninsula that Halifax occupies, is a particularly attractive piece of greenery, whose beach and shady woods make it perfect for picnics. The park is also popular with joggers and hikers, and provides a fine vantage point from which to watch the big ships in the harbour and the yachts on the Northwest Arm.

Situated among old ruined fortifications is the **Prince of Wales Tower** (daily July–Aug 9am–5pm) built by Prince Edward in 1796 and still intact. The tower, one of five in Nova Scotia, was the first in a series of these circular stone sentinels to be constructed along the coasts of North America and the British Isles. They were used as barracks, for weapon storage and as artillery platforms.

In the **Fairview Cemetery**, on the northwest side of town, are the graves of numerous victims of the *Titanic* ocean liner, which sank to the south of Newfoundland in 1912.

At the other end of Halifax, is **Fort Needham Park**, created in memory of the tragedy of 6 December 1917, commonly known as the Halifax explosion. On that day, a French munitions ship, the *Mont Blanc*, loaded with a cargo of ammunition and explosives, collided with another ship in Halifax harbour. The massive explosion that followed killed 2,000 outright and injured thousands more. Half the city was destroyed in what is said to have been the biggest man-made blast prior to the Hiroshima bomb in 1945.

Pier 21 National Historic Site (May–Oct daily 9.30am–5.30pm, Nov–Apr Tue–Sat 10am–5pm) overlooks Halifax Harbour. As Canada's last surviving ocean immigration shed, it presents the stories of one million people who arrived here between 1928 and 1971 – recounting the emotional experiences of the immigrants, war brides, displaced children and Canadian military troops who passed through its doors.

Halifax Public Gardens

Dartmouth

Across the harbour from Halifax is **Dartmouth**. Although known for its industry, it has 25 sparkling lakes on which locals enjoy fishing and canoeing in summer and skating in winter. Founded in 1750, when British troops from across the harbour came on woodcutting expeditions, it developed largely in response to Halifax's needs, and in 1752 it began operating a ferry between the two settlements. The boats still ply the harbour, in what is the oldest saltwater ferry service in North America.

Quakers from Nantucket Island settled here between 1785 and 1792, after the American Revolution. They made Dartmouth the headquarters of a whaling company whose operations were centred at what is now the **Dartmouth Shipyards.** They also left behind a number of houses, many of which still stand. These simple structures were built to endure; a stroll down Ochterloney

Acadian church of St Mary's

tants is an attractive town of grey-weathered shingle-board houses. The city is proud to have built the original *Bluenose* racing schooner in 1921. Champion of four international schooner races, it is portrayed on the Canadian 10-cent coin. A faithful replica still uses Lunenburg as its home base, when it is not cruising along the Atlantic coast, and is open to visitors when in port. You can even take a two-hour cruise. 'Bluenose' was an American nickname for Nova Scotia's wind-whipped sailors.

On the waterfront, the **Fisheries Museum of the Atlantic** (mid-May–June and Sept–mid-Oct daily 9.30am–5.30pm, July–Aug Sun–Mon 9.30am–5.30pm, Tue–Sat 9.30am–7pm, mid-Oct–mid-May Mon–Fri 9am–4pm) will give you a vivid sense of the history of sailing and fishing along Nova Scotia's coasts. Besides a model of the *Bluenose*, the museum's star attractions are two old ships moored in the port: the schooner *Theresa E. Connor*, used for cod fishing, and the trawler *Cape Sable*. Across the harbour, walk over the cliffs to **The Ovens**. These caves were the scene of a mini gold rush in 1861, when New Englanders poured into the area to pan nuggets from the shale on the beach.

Annapolis Valley

Highway 101 takes you from Halifax northwest across the peninsula through the apple orchards, strawberry fields and cattle pastures of **Annapolis Valley's** farmland. This is the heart of Nova Scotia's French Acadia. In spring the scent of apple blossom lingers in the air, and the **Apple Blossom Festival** is celebrated.

In Windsor, stop off to see the 18th-century blockhouse at **Fort Edward** (named after Governor Edward Cornwallis), a grim monument to the British military presence that forced the Acadians to leave their lands. The dispersal began at **Grand-Pré**, now a national historic site (mid-May–mid-Oct daily 9am–6pm) commemorating the Acadians' resilience. At the time, this was the centre of a thriving farming community that built dykes to reclaim marshland, grew fruit and vegetables, and raised animals. The farms were destroyed by the British in 1704. In 1747, the French gained the upper hand, but only for eight years. The 2,000-strong community was expelled, to return a few years later and re-establish their farms all over again. A stone church was erected in the park in 1930 as a memorial to Acadian culture and history. The bronze statue in the gardens is Evangeline, tragic heroine of Henry Longfellow's 1847 poem of the same name about the deportation. Along the Annapolis River road, such

Bitter-Sweet Acadia

Before the British came, the region of the Maritimes was known as Acadia, a corruption of Arcadia – the 'Peaceful Land' of the Ancient Greeks – which the 16th-century Italian explorer Giovanni da Verrazzano thought he had rediscovered. The first French colonists settled here in the 1600s to farm the rich soil and fish the waters.

But trouble began in 1621, when Edinburgh-born King James I of England authorised traders to colonise the land, which they renamed New Scotland (Nova Scotia). This strategic zone between New France and New England was swapped back and forth until the 1713 Treaty of Utrecht handed Acadia to England. The Acadians claimed neutrality, and refused to fight against the French.

The lieutenant governor of Nova Scotia organised the deportation of some 10,000 men, women and children, scattering them across North America. Some ended up in Louisiana, where their descendants are known as Cajuns. The upheaval was known as *le Grand Dérangement* (the Great Disturbance or Disruption). Today the Acadians number some 300,000, and their largest community is in New Brunswick.

pretty little villages as **Middleton**, **Lawrencetown** and **Bridgetown** bear the unmistakable mark of the New Englanders who moved into the region to take over the Acadians' farms.

On the estuary, the peaceful town of **Annapolis Royal** was the scene of 14 sieges (by the English and the French) and countless pirate raids. Formerly Port Royal, it was renamed after England's Queen Anne and became capital of Nova Scotia until the foundation of Halifax. **Fort Anne** (daily mid-May–mid-Oct 9am–5.30pm, July–Aug until 6pm) is now a pleasant park of grassy knolls and ridges, the remains of the earthwork defences. Only a powder house in the southwest bastion and a storehouse in the northwest survive. The officers' quarters, built in 1797, have been reconstructed to house a museum on local First Nations culture. In the **Annapolis Royal Historic Gardens** (daily May–June and Sept–Oct 9am–5pm, July–Aug 9am–8pm), south of the city centre, each local population group is honoured by a display of flowers: mayflowers and pines for the Mi'kmaq; irises for the Acadians, plus the vegetables they grew (their ingenious system of dykes is reconstructed, as is a typical Acadian cottage); and an English rose arbour and Victorian flower beds. A **marsh lookout** gives good views over the estuary. In the town centre, the shops and taverns on **Lower St George Street** are being transformed to recapture the town's Victorian era.

Port Royal (10km/6 miles west along Highway 1; mid-May–mid-Oct daily 9am–5.30pm, July–Aug until 6pm) is a fine recreation of Samuel de Champlain's timbered **Habitation**, built in 1608. Furniture, utensils and craftware, supplemented by audiovisual shows, give a vivid insight into the earliest permanent European settlement north of Florida. You can see how the French settlers made friendly contact with the Mi'kmaq; and hear how Champlain kept up morale during the long winters with the first Canadian social club, the Order of Good Cheer (each member would organise a fortnightly banquet of game and fish he had caught himself) and the first Canadian dramatic production, *Le Théâtre de Neptune*, by the colony's lawyer, Marc Lescarbot.

A moose on the leafy slopes of Cape Breton Highlands
National Park

Cape Breton Island

Cape Breton Island has always been a place apart – occupied
by the French longer than the rest of Nova Scotia (they called it
Ile Royale) and a separate province until 1820. The Canso
Causeway to the mainland, was not constructed until 1955.

❶

The airport outside Sydney, the island's largest town, is the
most convenient gateway for both the Fortress of Louisbourg
National Historic Park to the east and the Cabot Trail to the
west, leading to Cape Breton Highlands National Park.

To get to Louisbourg you may like to take the more round-
about coast road. On the way, take the time to visit **Glace Bay**
and the **Cape Breton Miners' Museum** (June–Oct daily 10am–
6pm, July–Aug Tue until 7pm, Nov–May Mon–Fri 9am–4pm),
one of Nova Scotia's finest. Artefacts and photographs chroni-
cle the history of coal mining in the town and commemorate the
men who risked their lives working in the depths. You travel
along the shafts and galleries of the abandoned Ocean Deep

Mine, which reaches 13km (8 miles) out and 800m (2,625ft) under the Atlantic. Coal has been mined in the vicinity of Glace Bay since the 18th century, when soliders from nearby Louisbourg were assigned this duty. Weary from your exertions, you can have a coal miner's meal at the colliery canteen.

⑮ The great French fortress town of **Louisbourg** (daily mid-May–Oct 9.30am–5pm, Nov–mid-May 8am–4pm), a national historic park, is one of the best examples in Canada's programme of historical reconstructions. You'll need a full day to do it justice. After the guided tour, take time to discuss details of 18th-century French colonial life with the costumed volunteers performing the roles of fishermen, merchants, soldiers and craftspeople.

Building of the original fortress began in 1719, six years after the Treaty of Utrecht had left the French with only Cape Breton Island. The ice-free port provided year-round defence for access to the Gulf of St Lawrence and Québec, and a commercial base for cod fishing, trade with the Caribbean and smuggling to and from New England. The reconstruction of one-fifth of the town recaptures life as it was in the summer of 1744, a year before the first great British siege and 16 years before its destruction.

A fleur de lys on the door of Porte Dauphine

As soon as you arrive at the Georges des Roches fishery you are plunged into the atmosphere of that time. At the turf-roofed log cabin outside the walls, dozens of cod are put out to dry on the same trestled wooden racks still used in fishing villages all down the coast.

At the drawbridge to **Porte Dauphine**, the main entrance gate, French soldiers will stop you to check whether you're a British spy. If they let you through (they usually do), walk past the Dauphin bastion to the handsomely carved stone gate, **Porte Frédéric**. Turn right into the town along the main street.

At the Hôtel de la Marine and Grandchamps Inn you will be served an 18th-century

meal, dished up on tin or pewter plates; fine meals are served more traditionally at L'Epée Royale.

Continue to the **King's Bastion**, the military barracks where the stark living conditions led to a mutiny in 1744. The gabled Governor's Wing contains 10 luxurious apartments with fine furniture, tapestries, silks, brocades, silverware and porcelain. The adjacent Officers' Quarters are more humble but comfortable enough, while the ordinary soldiers' barracks are downright miserable, with rudimentary beds of straw. In the middle of the block, a simple little chapel tries to keep the peace.

Back in Sydney, follow the Trans-Canada Highway west to the Englishtown exit for the ferry across St Ann's Bay to join the **Cabot Trail** at Indian Brook. This 300km (186-mile) trail, named after the explorer John Cabot, offers one of the country's most spectacular drives, with dramatic juxtapositions of dense pine forest, sheer cliffs and the ocean.

Travel north along the **Gaelic Coast** – a name that is amply justified by the thick Scottish burr you'll hear from most of the (very friendly) people you speak to on the way.

Ingonish is a popular resort town on two bays with fine sandy beaches, offering excellent sailing, fishing and swimming. Have a drink at the Keltic Lodge Resort & Spa, an old Nova Scotia landmark that is worth a visit for its view of Cape Smokey.

Cape Breton Highlands National Park is a joy for nature-lovers. The Cabot Trail leads you around the periphery, but well-marked hiking trails (maps are available at the Ingonish park entrance) take you into the interior. Among the most interesting trails, the best are the Glasgow Lakes trail to John Deer Lake and the trail around Beulach Ban Falls and French Mountain.

Camping facilities on the edge of the park are better equipped than those in the forest. These 'New Scottish' highlands look uncannily like those in the old country. A Scottish shepherd's cottage, **Lone Shieling**, off the highway at Grande Anse River, reinforces the impression.

The forest, a mixture of conifers and hardwoods, shelters white-tailed deer, black bears, moose, beavers, red foxes, lynx, mink and snowshoe hares. Bird-watchers can spot, among the many species, red-tailed hawks and the occasional bald eagle. Anglers should obtain a permit at one of the park's information centres to fish for trout or salmon (no motorboats are allowed). On the northeast corner of the park, **Neil Harbour** is a pleasant little fishing port with sandy beaches.

To explore the northern tip of the island, leave the park at South Harbour and drive 16km (10 miles) to the fishing village of **Bay St Lawrence**. Take a bracing walk along the grassy clifftop west of town, but beware of the winds. Southwest of the park, **Chéticamp** is an old Acadian stronghold. Be sure to visit **Les Trois Pignons**, a cultural and information centre that houses two fascinating museums. The Elizabeth LeFort Museum features the permanent collection of a master artist in wool, and the Musée Marguerite Gallant displays antiques and artefacts collected during the lifetime of its namesake.

Anglers insist that the salmon fishing near **Margaree Forks** is the best in eastern Canada. North East Margaree has a **salmon museum** (daily mid-June–mid-Oct 9am–5pm) devoted to the fish and the cunning tricks used by poachers.

In a setting of wooded hills around Bras d'Or (Golden Arm) Lake, **Baddeck** is where the inventor of the telephone, Alexander Graham Bell, chose to spend the last, very active years of his life. His home, hidden in the forest, is not open to the public.

The marvellously organised museum set in the **Alexander Gra-**

ham Bell National Historic Park (daily May–mid Oct) shows how the great man devoted his energies in Baddeck to aviation. Besides his invention of the tetrahedral kite, the exhibits illustrate his work on the telephone and inventions of medical and maritime instruments. The museum devotes plenty of space to photographs of Bell's family life in Edinburgh, the United States and Baddeck – which reminded him of the countryside near Edinburgh.

Hiking the Cabot Trail in Cape Breton Highlands National Park

If all this has whetted your appetite for things Scottish, you should end your tour at the southern tip of St Ann's Bay, where the **Gaelic College of Celtic Arts and Crafts** offers summer courses in playing the Highland bagpipes, Cape Breton fiddle, Celtic harp or Scottish small pipes, as well as pipe-band drumming and Highland dancing.

Even if you're not tempted to sign up, you can watch classes in progress. In August, the **Gaelic Mod** gathers Scots old and new for Gaelic cultural events, highland-dance competitions and evening ceilidhs.

Prince Edward Island

Canada's smallest province, just 224km (139 miles) long and only 64km (40 miles) across at its widest point, has a gentle rural atmosphere of rolling green meadows in the interior, with a coast of long sandy beaches at the foot of terracotta cliffs.

16 ▶ **Prince Edward Island** (PEI), nestles snugly in the Gulf of St Lawrence, separated from New Brunswick and Nova Scotia by the Northumberland Strait. More than three-quarters of the area is given over to farmland.

The red soil is best for potatoes, but farmers also grow blueberries, raspberries and strawberries. The island's lobsters are a worthy rival to Nova Scotia's, but it is the oysters of Malpeque Bay that are especially renowned.

Jacques Cartier named the island Ile St-Jean when he spotted it in the 16th century, but the French didn't colonise it until after their retrenchment following the 1713 Treaty of Utrecht. Like Nova Scotia, the island was transformed by the Acadians' deportation and their replacement by New Englanders, who named it after Prince Edward, Duke of Kent, in 1799. The New Englanders preferred to exploit their property as absentee landlords, leaving it mainly to Irish and Scottish immigrants to clear the forests for shipbuilding and agriculture.

Prince Edward Island's great historical moment came in 1864, when its capital, Charlottetown, hosted a meeting of Maritime leaders, with delegates from Ontario and Québec, to chart the path to Canada's federal status as a united dominion. Since 1997, Confederation Bridge has connected PEI (at Borden-Carleton) with Cape Jourimain in New Brunswick. Despite fears that the island would lose its distinct character, the bridge has certainly boosted tourism.

Tourism, along with agriculture and fishing, are the island's main industries. The superb sandy beaches of the north coast attract more than half a million visitors a year. Fans of Lucy Maud Montgomery's novel, *Anne of Green Gables*, can visit the house and the landscape in which it was set *(see page 142)*.

After visiting centrally located Charlottetown, you can take three well-marked scenic drives around the island: Blue Heron Coastal Drive in the centre, North Cape Coastal Drive to the west, and Points East Coastal Drive to the east, corresponding roughly to the three counties, Queens, Prince and Kings.

The red sandstone cliffs of Prince Edward Island

Charlottetown

The island's low-key charm is reflected in its capital city (population 32,000). Named after the wife of George III of England, **Charlottetown** offers a colourful mix of greenery and Victorian-style buildings in red stone. It's a busy port, a commercial and tourist centre, but remains resolutely old-fashioned.

Starting in Confederation Plaza, visit **Province House** (mid-Oct–May Mon–Fri 9am–5pm, June–mid-Oct daily 9am–5pm), the sober grey sandstone Georgian building in which the 'Fathers of the Confederation' met in 1864. (Ironically, Prince Edward Island was at first hesitant to join Canada, and did not enter the Confederation until 1873.) Built in 1847, it is now the seat of the provincial legislature. **Confederation Chamber** has been restored with the names of the august delegates.

Next door stands the **Confederation Centre of the Arts** opened in 1964 to commemorate the Confederation Conference's centenary. The complex includes a museum, an art gallery and theatre. Inside the gallery is the work of 19th-century PEI portraitist

The blue heron has given its name to a tourist circuit

Robert Harris, celebrated for his group picture of the Fathers of the Confederation. Each summer the arts centre hosts the Charlottetown Festival, Canada's best-known music and theatre festival, which runs from mid-June to early October. On Kent Street you'll find **Beaconsfield Historic House** a Victorian mansion and once one of Charlottetown's finest residences.

Blue Heron Coastal Drive

The 190km (118-mile) circuit follows the north shore, with its barrier islands, windswept dunes, red cliffs and salt marshes, then around to the Northumberland Strait. From Charlottetown, head north to the great beaches of **Prince Edward Island National Park**. The north shore's amazingly warm water (22°C/72°F in summer) offers the balmiest bathing in the Maritimes.

The park includes the most popular attraction on the whole island, **Green Gables House** (May–Oct daily 9am–5pm), a neat white-frame farmhouse with green shutters. Lucy Maud Montgomery (1874–1942) lived here as a child and later used it as the setting for her novel, *Anne of Green Gables*. Here, Montgomery's typewriter is displayed.

North Cape Coastal Drive

Starting out from Summerside, this 288km (179-mile) western circuit around Prince County takes you through the Acadian community (close to 3,000) living on the south coast around Egmont Bay. Many of the villages fly the Acadians' blue, white and red flag modelled on that of France, but with a single star added to the blue band.

Just west of Summerside, visit the **Miscouche Acadian Museum** (Sept–June Mon–Fri 9.30am–5pm, Sun 1–4pm, July–Aug daily 9.30am–7pm). The island's 19th-century shipbuilding industry is featured in **Green Park Shipbuilding Museum** at Port Hill. Gourmets head straight for the renowned oysters of Malpeque Bay. Out in the bay, on Lennox Island, is a settlement of Mi'kmaq Indians.

Points East Coastal Drive

East of Charlottetown, the longest of the circuits, the 411km (255-mile) **Points East Coastal Drive** encompasses pleasant beaches, rugged, red-stone capes and coves, shady forests, lobster and tuna fisheries and potato and fruit farms.

The **Orwell Corner Historic Village** (late May–June Mon–Fri 9am–4.30pm, July–Aug daily 9.30am–5.30pm, Sept–early Oct Mon–Fri 9am–4.30pm) includes original log cabins built in the early 1800s. Most of the early settlers here were Scottish and in summer the sounds of the Highlands can be enjoyed at a weekly *ceilidh*, an evening of Scottish music and dancing.

Anne of Greenbacks

Cavendish, west of Robinson's Island, is the centre of *Anne of Green Gables* country. Fans of the novel by Lucy Maud Montgomery, published in 1908 and translated into 30 languages, and its many sequels, flock to visit the lovely Green Gables house itself as well as the author's birthplace (Clifton, New London); the Green Gables Post Office (Cavendish); Anne's 'House of Dreams' (French River), and Anne of Green Gables Museum at Park Corner. In summer, the Charlottetown Festival presents a musical comedy based on the original novel.

In 1803 a Scotsman by the name of Lord Selkirk financed the emigration of three shiploads of impoverished Highlanders, who had lost their land in the Highland Clearances, to Prince Edward Island. The 'Selkirk Pioneers' settled in Eldon, 13km (8 miles) south of Orwell, and today a restoration and reconstruction, the **Lord Selkirk Pioneer Settlement**, provides insight into their existence. It is one of the largest collections of authentic log buildings in Canada. The clans gather in Eldon every year in early August for the Highland Games.

Other sights on the island include the **Basin Head Fisheries Museum** (daily mid-June–Sept) at its eastern end, and tells the story of PEI's historic inshore fishery through displays, exhibits and dioramas. On the north shore, at North Lake, boats can be chartered for deep-sea fishing.

New Brunswick

With its rugged coastline and huge forests that cover 85 percent of its territory, the province of **New Brunswick** attracts nature-loving campers as well as fishermen and hunters. Anglers can hope for trout, bass, pickerel and salmon, while hunters go for the duck and grouse. Wildlife enthusiasts may be lucky enough to see white-tailed deer, black bears and moose in the forests. In the Bay of Fundy you can observe at your leisure the remarkable effects in the river estuaries and along the coast produced by the 16m (52ft) high tides, which are particularly evident at the Hopewell Rocks, at Hopewell Cape.

Linked to Nova Scotia by the Chignecto Isthmus, New Brunswick became a separate province in 1784 at the demand of 14,000 Loyalist refugees. It took its name from the German duchy then ruled by George III of England. The Loyalists joined earlier settlers from New England, Pennsylvania and Yorkshire, and the French Acadians who had come back after their deportation in the Anglo-French wars.

Today, New Brunswick is Canada's only bilingual province; one-third of the population speaks French.

Kayaking at Nictau Lake, New Brunswick

Saint John

The province's largest town (where it is the custom never to abbreviate 'Saint' to 'St') is in the Bay of Fundy, at the mouth of the Saint John River. It is the centre of a paper and pulp industry and has the largest oil refinery in Canada, but the city fathers have worked miracles to beautify the waterfront.

One of the town's main attractions is the natural phenomenon of the Bay of Fundy's extraordinary tides, with a variation from low to high tide of 8.5m (26ft) at the mouth of the Saint John River. Watch the **Reversing Falls Rapids** from the park on Bridge Street. The tourist information office there will tell you the best times to watch this extraordinary phenomenon. At low tide, the Fundy's waters are 4m (13ft) lower than the Saint John River, causing it to cascade through a narrow gorge into the bay. Gradually the flow slows down as the tide begins to rise again. At the tide's turn, the slack enables ships to pass the rapids into the Saint John River before the flow builds up in the opposite direction. The bay's high tide thrusts all the way inland to Fredericton, 130km (80

Whale watching off the Bay of Fundy

miles) away. If you want to explore the Bay of Fundy, take a stroll in the **Irving Nature Park** on the west side of the city or along **Harbour Passage**, an interconnected system of walking trails, lookouts and heritage sites extending along the inner harbour.

The bright new city centre area blends 19th-century and modern styles, especially along red-brick **King Street**. To suit all weathers, the 'Inside Connection' links entertainment and shopping centres. **Market Square** is the revitalised downtown waterfront district: old warehouses have been transformed into a complex of shops, apartments, hotels, cafés and the New Brunswick Museum. At nearby **Barbour's General Store** (mid-June–mid-Oct daily 9am–6pm), an authentic 19th-century grocery, try the local speciality of dulse, a seaweed that is New Brunswick's answer to chewing gum. It was at Market Slip that a contingent of 3,000 Loyalists landed in 1783 to found the city of Saint John.

New Brunswick Museum (1 Market Square; Mon–Fri 9am–5pm, Thur until 9pm, Sat 10am–5pm, Sun noon–5pm) is devoted principally to the province's shipbuilding industry, the source of considerable prosperity before timber had to give way to the new age of steel. There are also interesting exhibits on the life of the Mi'kmaq First Nation and the Bay of Fundy's tides. The collection of local artefacts ranges from a 13,000-year-old mastodon tooth to a gold-plated cornet.

Bay of Fundy

Take Route 1 northeast from Saint John and turn off at exit 211 onto Route 114 to head for **Fundy National Park**, a wonderful nature reserve bordering the seashore with its spectacular high tides. At the park entrance you can get detailed maps of the 110km (68 miles) of hiking and biking trails linking camp sites and chalets inside the park. The park organises a number of family-oriented activities, such as the popular 'beach crawl' at low tide, guided walks through the forest and evening programmes at the outdoor theatre. On Bennett Lake, you can hire a canoe or fish from a rowing boat. On the shore, walk along the flats at low tide to seek out periwinkles, barnacles and sea anemones underneath the rocks.

Make a detour to **Hopewell Cape** on Route 114, which will give you a good view and explanations of the bay's tidal phenomena *(see pages 144–5)*. If possible, camp overnight: dawn is the perfect time to enjoy the view of the red cliffs and granite pillars topped with tufts of balsam fir and black spruce, revealed at low tide. In St Martins, on Route 111, the **Fundy Trail** offers spectacular views, whether you're driving, cycling, kayaking or walking.

Fredericton

New Brunswick's riverfront capital is a pleasing blend of heritage, architecture, thriving arts and craft-making traditions. Riverboat cruises (daily in summer) are a good way to enjoy the cityscape from a different perspective. The splendid **Beaverbrook Art Gallery** (June–mid-Oct daily 9am–5.30pm, Thur until 9pm, Sun noon–5.30pm, mid-Oct–June Tue– Sun) was built by William Maxwell Aitken (1879–1964) who, as Lord Beaverbrook, became a British press baron and a member of Winston Churchill's war cabinet in World War II. The gallery has an imposing portrait, by Gra-

Elms and pewter

Fredericton is known as 'the City of Stately Elms' as it has a number of these fine trees. The town is also held to be the pewter capital of Canada due to its widely acclaimed pewtersmiths.

is not true, for example, that the icebergs you may see off St John's in the spring are styrofoam structures towed out for decoration by the Chamber of Commerce, although locals may tell you otherwise. In fact, the best place to see icebergs is around St Anthony's, on the island's northern tip.

St John's

Folklore insists that the name (not to be confused with Saint John, New Brunswick) comes from the saint's day of John the Baptist, 24 June, when John Cabot is said to have arrived here in 1497. Newfoundland and Labrador's capital and largest city retains the allure of the fishing port it has always been. However, as a now booming offshore oil capital, you will find plenty of choice when it comes to hotels and excellent restaurants.

The picturesque **harbour** is the place to begin an exploration. In the 19th century the town burned down five times, but people still stubbornly built wooden houses overlooking the water-

Colourful houses in Newfoundland

front. Their brightly painted walls offset the gaunt grey trawlers in the docks. The old buildings on **Water Street**, which dates to the 16th century and may be North America's oldest street, have been converted into trendy boutiques and art galleries. Parallel to the harbour, on **Gower Street**, you'll find the prettiest Victorian houses, painted burgundy, lemon, burnt sienna, dove grey and white. Still around the waterfront, the downtown bar scene is booming.

At 9 Bonaventure Avenue, **The Rooms** (June–mid-Oct Mon–Sat 10am–5pm, Wed until 9pm, Sun noon–5pm, mid-Oct–May closed Mon) house the provincial museum, art gallery and archives in a striking building based on the buildings and shoreline structures found in outport Newfoundland and Labrador. The museum recounts the human history of the island, exploring the changes and connections, and how nature interwove with the lives of the peoples who lived here from 9,000 years ago to 1730, as well as exhibiting the clothing, furniture and implements of the first European fishermen.

Safely up on a hill on Military Road, the Catholic **Basilica of St John the Baptist** (1850) escaped the numerous fires to dominate the town's skyline with its granite and limestone towers. Down on Gower Street, the **Anglican Cathedral**, also named after John the Baptist, burned down twice, and the simple, neo-Gothic, 20th-century version is still without a steeple.

The summit of **Signal Hill** offers the best panorama of the harbour overlooking The Narrows and out to the Atlantic Ocean. The hill was fortified to guard the harbour entrance during the Napoleonic Wars, and you can still see cannon of the Queen's Battery, installed in 1796. The **Cabot Tower** at the top of the hill was built in 1897, marking the fourth centenary of Cabot's landing and the diamond jubilee of Queen Victoria. Four years later, at 12.30pm, 12 December 1901, in a receiving station improvised near the tower in a hospital (burned down in 1920), the Italian inventor Guglielmo Marconi picked up the first transatlantic wireless message, three faint dots of the letter S in Morse, from his transmitter in Poldhu, in Cornwall, England. The event is commemorated by a modest exhibit in the Cabot Tower.

On the north side of the hill, **Quidi Vidi** is a charming fishing port. On the first Wednesday in August, the Royal St John's Regatta, a race for six-oar rowing boats, is held on Quidi Vidi Lake; it is also the occasion of a boisterous garden party.

Avalon Peninsula

The drive south down the peninsula from St John's takes you first out to **Cape Spear**, the most easterly point of both Newfoundland and the continent (longitude 52°37'24'). This strategic position prompted the Americans to install two gun emplacements on the tip of the cape in World War II. The 1835 white clapboard **lighthouse** here has been restored with a jolly red-and-white striped dome, while a less-attractive modern concrete tower does all the work. Down at the seabird sanctuary on **Witless Bay**, you can spot Atlantic puffins, black-legged kittiwake and thick-billed murre. The best time for sightings is from mid-June to mid-July, when you can hire a boat from Bay Bulls out to the four islands – **Gull**, **Green**, **Pee Pee** and **Great** – of the ecological reserve.

Marine Drive, which follows the craggy coast north of St John's, passes through the fishing villages of Outer Cove, Mid-

Talking Newfoundland English

If you remember that St John's is closer to Ireland than Toronto, you won't be surprised by the spoken language in Newfoundland: a unique blend of dialects from England's West Country and southwest Ireland, brought over by the original settlers and unchanged for centuries. It is the closest dialect in the modern world to Shakespearean English, and the only place where many words and expressions that were common in the 17th century still survive. As the local proverb has it, 'you can't tell the mind of a squid' (meaning 'beware of unreliable people') and 'long may your big jib draw' – 'good luck'!

dle Cove and Torbay up to pretty Pouch Cove. In summer, whales pass down this coast on their way south.

Two World Heritage Sites

On the west coast of the island's Northern Peninsula, 30km (19 miles) north of Deer Lake on Highway 430, **Gros Morne National Park** lies within the Long Range Mountains. The 1,800-sq-km (700-sq-mile) national park has some of the most dramatic scenery in eastern Canada. Its geological features uniquely illustrate movements of the earth's crust and its mountains were sculpted by Ice-Age glaciers that cut deep fjords (called ponds in Newfoundland) and

Exploring the fjords in Gros Morne National Park

valleys. Dominating the landscape is Gros Morne Mountain, a huge rock that emerged molten from between the earth's surface plates and then toppled over. Elsewhere in the park are bogs, sand dunes and 70km (44 miles) of coastline. The park is a meeting place for three ecological zones – arctic alpine, boreal and temperate – and a wonderful place to hike or fish for salmon and trout. There is an interpretive centre close to **Rocky Harbour**, a fishing village.

At the tip of the northern peninsula, **L'Anse aux Meadows National Historic Site** (daily June–early Oct 9am–6pm) is the location of the only authenticated Viking settlement in the New World. It is believed to have been the site of Lief Ericson's colony following his landing around AD1000. The park's replicated sod and stone houses and workshops give a fair idea of conditions a thousand years ago. An excellent interpretation centre contains archaeological specimens and audio-visual presentations.

BRITISH COLUMBIA

'Such a land,' said Rudyard Kipling in 1908, 'is good for an energetic man. It is also not bad for a loafer.' That's still true today. **British Columbia**, the third largest province, is supremely the land of the wild outdoors, with the constant challenge of rugged mountains, seemingly impenetrable forests, a jagged coastline and fast-moving rivers. Its capital, Victoria, is a lively university town offering cutting-edge theatre, great jazz and a plethora of micro-breweries that produce some of Canada's best ales. Vancouver, with a population of around 600,000, is the principal city of the province. Beautifully situated, it offers easy living, elegant architecture, and all the excitement of an international port.

Wildlife in Vancouver

Long after the Aboriginal Peoples had settled the area, British fur traders discovered and began to exploit this land of plenty, which they named New Caledonia. Gold discovered in 1858 on the Fraser River attracted many adventurers, and Britain decided it was time to take over the land from the Hudson's Bay Company and create the colony of British Columbia. It joined the

Dominion of Canada in 1871, on the understanding that it would be linked to the Canadian Pacific Railway within the next decade (delay nearly caused secession). The terminus of the Canadian Pacific, Vancouver, is British Columbia's most important port.

King of the salmon

On Vancouver Island, the salmon swim upstream to their breeding grounds. The chinook, which can weigh up to 57kg (126lb), is the king of all the Pacific salmon.

The greatest attractions of this province are its incredible natural beauty and its climate: gentle, relatively dry summers and mild (but rainy) winters, at least in the southwest corner, where three-quarters of the population live. When it comes to the economy, about half of all the goods produced here are forestry products. The spruce, fir and cedar provide much of Canada's construction lumber and considerable quantities of wood pulp and paper.

Much to the joy of sports fishermen, salmon remains another great natural resource of the rivers and the Pacific coast. In a province where revenues from hydroelectric power are second only to those of Québec, the energy industry has been prevented from damming the River Fraser in order to protect the salmon's spawning grounds.

British Columbia's population of 4.5 million is concentrated around the Strait of Georgia and along the US border, with hardly any inhabitants at all north of Prince Rupert. The majority (but steadily decreasing) are of British origin. Other European immigrants are German, Dutch, Greek, Ukrainian, Italian, Scandinavian and a few French. The Aboriginal Peoples number about 196,000. In addition, there are important Chinese, Japanese and, more recently, Vietnamese, Korean, East Indian and Pakistani communities.

Vancouver

The city's setting in a magnificent bay embraced by soaring green mountains is one of those blessings that can turn an atheist into a believer. Cynicism dissolves with your first taste of the gentle atmosphere of **Vancouver**, created by a combination of the comforts of sophisticated modernity with the simpler joys of the wilderness so close at hand. Expanding at a purposeful but more leisurely pace than other leading Canadian cities such as Toronto and Calgary, Vancouver has never lost sight of the importance of enjoying life. Perhaps Vancouver being Canada's most expensive city for buying property is a reflection of that.

In keeping with this easy-going attitude, the city was originally known as Gastown, after saloon-keeper 'Gassy Jack' Deighton, who looked after the needs of pioneer lumbermen and sailors in the 1860s. It was only when the town became the Canadian Pacific Railway's West Coast terminus in 1886 that it took on the more dignified name of one of the region's first European visitors, navigator George Vancouver. A fire in 1886 and subsequent property development left few traces of the 19th-century town, but bold contemporary architecture downtown and out at the Simon Fraser and University of British Columbia campuses blends beautifully with the mountain and ocean backdrop. Unsightly docklands have been cleaned up, and handsome new housing built on the waterfront.

Overview

Vancouver's exceptional setting has always been difficult to appreciate in its entirety. The city stretches along the banks of the huge English Bay on the one side and of Burrard Inlet on the other, which George Vancouver explored in a scouting boat in 1792. The harbour and the Stanley Park promontory separate the city from its residential suburbs of West and North Vancouver. To take all this in you need to begin from two observation points.

Cross the First Narrows on Lion's Gate Bridge and take the Capilano Road to the Skyride for a cable-car ride to the top of **Grouse Mountain**. You will have a superb view over the city and harbour. Aim to be there at sunset, to see the city light up. To the northwest the mountain (a favourite with skiers) over-

View of Vancouver from the North Shore

looks Capilano Lake and across to Vancouver Island. On your
way back turn off to walk the swaying suspension bridge 70m
(230ft) above the fast-flowing waters of **Capilano Canyon**.

Back in the town centre, go to the panoramic terrace on top of
the 50-storey **Vancouver Lookout at Harbour Centre** (555 West
Hastings Street). The beauty of the city set against the mountains
is breathtaking. On clear days, using a telescope, the view extends
as far south as Mount Baker, in the state of Washington, in the US.

For tourist information about the province, go to the City of
Vancouver Visitor Centre on the plaza level of 200 Burrard
Street. There is also a visitor centre at Vancouver International
Airport and more than 100 scattered throughout the province.

Downtown

Georgia and Robson streets are the main arteries that run through
the West End peninsula to Stanley Park. Georgia Street continues
through the park to Lion's Gate Bridge. Leave your car parked
safely and visit the city centre on foot – the traffic jams can be ter-

Lions Gate bridge

rible. Start your tour of downtown Vancouver at Robson Square, site of the **Courthouse**. Designed by Arthur Erickson, it is one of the masterpieces of contemporary North American architecture. The building, characteristic of the Vancouver architect's work, is horizontal, and only seven storeys high. Yet it is the main focus in the square, despite the skyscrapers towering above it. Here there are no marble columns or porticos – features that grace traditional law court buildings. Instead, the structure spreads out in tiers of glassed-in walkways, offices and courtrooms, shops and restaurants. Water from pools cascades from one level to the next among the gardens of flowering shrubs and rose bushes, orange trees, Japanese maples and a miniature pine forest. A pattern of stairways and ramps collectively dubbed 'stramps' – popular with roller-bladers – runs across the plazas from corner to corner, attracting crowds who gather here during city celebrations.

Robson Square also provides a home for the **Vancouver Art Gallery** (daily 10am–5pm Tue until 9pm) in the old courthouse – a neoclassical temple renovated by Erickson. Among the collection of works by Canadian artists on show are some by Emily Carr (1871–1945). 'Crazy Old Millie', as she was known locally – 'Klee Wyck' or the 'Laughing One' to her Kwakiutl Indian friends – was a popular eccentric in Victoria, where she kept a boarding house and wheeled a pet monkey around in a baby's pushchair. The years she spent painting among the First Nations and studying with French Post-Impressionists produced a unique style of vigorous, expressive landscapes and totemic themes, achieved with great sweeps and swirls of bold colour. Note in particular the lush, dramatic *Big Raven* (1931) and the haunting *Totem Forest* (1930).

The section of Robson Street between Burrard and Bute streets is especially cosmopolitan, packed with Vietnamese, Japanese, Scandinavian, Italian and French restaurants.

East of Robson Square, the **Granville Mall** pedestrian shopping zone takes you down to the Harbour Centre and the waterfront. From the foot of Granville Street, take a bargain cruise on the commuter **SeaBus**, which crosses Burrard Inlet to North Vancouver, 15 minutes each way. Besides the 'fish-eye view' of the city and harbour, you get a close-up of the grand **Canada Place**, jutting out into the harbour like an ocean liner, with a hint of the port's 19th-century beginnings in its white simulated sails. Originally the national pavilion at Expo '86, it is now the Vancouver Convention Centre.

Along Pender Street, **Chinatown** is Canada's largest Chinese community, mainly composed of the descendants of immigrants who worked on the Canadian Pacific Railway. Look for the fruit and vegetable markets, fish stalls, shops stocking spices and medicines, and boutiques selling silks and satins, bamboo and lacquer wares from Hong Kong, Taiwan and mainland China.

SeaBus crosses Burrard Inlet

Barbecued pork and poultry glisten in the windows of innumerable restaurants, and tourists are drawn in by the garish street décor.

Centre A, 2 West Hastings Street (Tue–Sat 11am–6pm), gives visitors the chance to delve deeper into the culture of Asia, with contemporary art and costumes, and photographs from China, Japan, India, Korea and Indonesia on show.

The **Dr Sun Yat-Sen Garden** (daily 10am–6pm), at the corner of Carrall and Pender streets, offers a rare moment of peace. A pavilion with glazed roof tiles, carved woodwork and lattice windows overlooks a subtly patterned, pebblestone courtyard and the miniature landscape. This microcosm of nature reflecting the Taoist philosophy of yin and yang was landscaped by artists brought in from Suzhou, the great centre of classical Chinese gardens. Light is balanced by shadow, and rugged limestone rocks (yang) are chosen for their pitted and convoluted surface, balancing the smooth surface of calm pools and quiet streams (yin). Shrubs symbolise human virtues: pine, bamboo and winter-blooming plum represent strength, grace and the renewal of life.

A stroll round Gastown

Duly refreshed, then, make your way towards the harbour and railyards, to **Gastown** (between Water and Hastings streets), the resuscitated red-brick, cobbled-street district of Vancouver's beginnings. This hucksters' paradise of boutiques, souvenir shops, bars, and restaurants is frankly commercial in its polished quaintness, but with a certain corny charm. Gastown takes its name from 'Gassy' Jack

Deighton, the area's premier barkeeper and self-proclaimed mayor. A former riverboat captain, Deighton opened a bar in the vicinity of the sawmills, within which drinking was forbidden. In Maple Tree Square, there is a statue of Deighton: he is standing on a barrel of whisky, thanks to which, according to legend, he persuaded lumbermen to build the town in 1867.

At the west end of Water Street is the world's first monumental **steam-powered clock**, signalling every 15 minutes with a resounding whistle.

If the Robson Square Courthouse whetted your appetite for more architecture by Arthur Erickson, continue by car or public transit out along Hastings Street towards Burnaby Mountain (actually only 400m/1,312ft high) and the striking campus of **Simon Fraser University**. The focus of student activity is the great mall of the extraordinary Academic Quadrangle, where light and shadow interplay delicately among stairways and terraces under the mall's truss-supported glass roof. On the way back downtown, swing over to the **BC Place**, a vast, concrete, oval-domed sports stadium, home to the BC Lions' and Vancouver Whitecaps' football teams.

Stanley Park

Situated on the peninsula dominating English Bay, **Stanley Park** is one of North America's finest city parks. The 405-hectare (1,000-acre) forest of Douglas firs, cedars and Sitka spruce were once a government reserve providing mast and spa timbers for the Royal Navy. In 1889, the city leased it as a park, named after Canada's governor general, Lord Stanley, the same man whose name stands for supremacy in professional hockey.

Early in the morning of 15 December 2006, a major windstorm struck this revered park with a vengeance. Thousands of trees were uprooted and its beloved 8.8km (5½-mile) **Seawall** promenade received major structural damage, necessitating an extremely long-term restoration programme. Nontheless, Stanley Park remains a 'must' on every visitor's itinerary.

Cricket in Stanley Park

You can walk, jog, or ride a bike (available for hire at nearby stores on Denman Street). Passing the immaculate green playing field of Brockton Oval, you may spot a cricket game, reminding you this is *British* Columbia. A splendid group of Haida and Kwakiutl totem poles nearby illustrate the province's other important cultural influence. On your way to Brockton Point, listen for the 9 o'clock gun, a cannon that fires at 9pm each evening, originally to warn fishermen of the fishing curfew.

Turning west along the seafront, you'll pass a bronze statue curiously named *Girl in a Wet Suit*, a version of Copenhagen's *Little Mermaid*, designed not to shock.

Further on, stop off at **Prospect Point** for a good view of oil tankers and grain cargo ships bound for Japan, China or Russia. A totem pole marks the site where Captain Vancouver met with members of the Squamish tribe.

At the **Vancouver Aquarium** (daily late June–early Sept 9.30am–7pm, early-Sept–late-June 9.30am–5pm) the star attractions are the dolphin show and the beluga whales, closely followed by sea otters and the archerfish feed programme. Look out for the wolf-eels, capable of cracking crabs with their jaws.

Marked trails lead to the pretty freshwater **Beaver Lake**, from which the beavers were 'deported' after creating havoc with the water system. The park's sandy **beaches** along the west shore of the peninsula are among the most popular in the area.

English Bay

Get away from the city centre with an excursion out to **Point Grey** where you can relax on the pleasant beaches (at Wreck Beach clothing is optional). The grounds of the **University of British Columbia**, one of the most beautiful college campuses in North America, are nearby; the terraced Sedgwick Library and the Faculty Club rose garden are two notable gems set against a superb sea and mountain backdrop.

On Marine Drive at Point Grey is the **Museum of Anthropology** (daily 10am–5pm, Tue until 9pm), is the pride of the university. In 1972, Arthur Erickson designed this noble glass-and-concrete-beam structure in homage to the post-and-beam longhouses of the Northwest Coast First Nations. Gracing the lawns are a magnificent group of **totem poles** and two **cedarwood houses** of the Haida Indians, built in the 1930s and faithful to a centuries-old technique and form.

The Raven and the First Men in the Museum of Anthropology

Inside the museum, alongside the artefacts of other Pacific civilisations, the rich culture of the coastal tribes – Haida, Kwakiutl, Salish, Tlingit and Tsimshian – is beautifully displayed and illuminated in a space where the roof-glass seems to open the halls to the heavens. Note the **cedarwood canoes**, built to negotiate the Pacific's coastal waters. Many of the **sculptures** you see were incorporated into the structure of a house as posts and crossbeams. One Kwakiutl giant accompanied by two slaves, emphasising the home-owner's power and prestige, originally supported a massive central roof beam. Others represent the tribes' totemic animals, such as the bear, protecting a human being in its bosom.

Prehistoric stone carvings show the continuity of totemic styles. Some smaller figures, in soft black argillite stone, were turned out by Haida craftsmen specifically for 19th-century European tourists who found themselves caricatured in the carvings. Notice the huge wooden feast dishes, as big as bathtubs, used for dispensing food at the great 'potlatch' ceremonies at which the tribes proclaimed their greatness by the munificence of their hospitality.

An important part of the collection is devoted to gold, silver and copper **jewellery**, and wooden **masks** and **ceremonial rattles**. Many of these are kept in the recently expanded Multiversity Galleries, in reality the museum's store rooms. This so-called **visible storage system** is a major innovation to make permanently available some 16,000 of the museum's art objects. Take full advantage of the system to make your own discoveries, to compare the work of different cultures around the world, or simply to admire the extraordinary richness of so-called 'primitive' art.

Just south of the museum, the **Nitobe Memorial Garden** (Mon–Fri 9am–5pm, Sat–Sun 9.30am–5pm) is a fine example of classical Japanese landscaping. The stone-lanterned paths lead across hump-bridged ponds to a traditional teahouse set among Japanese maples and azaleas.

Return to the city centre on Point Grey Road and stop off at the **Old Hastings Mill Store Museum** (1575 Alma Street; mid-June–mid-Sept Tue–Sun 11am–4pm, mid-Sept–mid-June Sat–Sun 1–4pm) near Jericho Beach. Carried here by barge in the 1930s, this is the town's oldest surviving building – a post office, general store and the only remnant from the original Gastown to have escaped the 1886 fire. Now fully restored, the building houses a museum for late-19th- and early 20th-century paraphernalia. **Kitsilano** was Vancouver's first bohemian neighbour-hood. Nowadays, those bohemians' counterparts, the students and artists, are more inclined to hang out on **Commercial Drive**.

In Vanier Park, near the Burrard Bridge, you'll find two small but interesting museums, and the Pacific Space Centre which houses the **HR MacMillan Space Centre** (daily July–Aug 10am–5pm, Sept–June Mon–Fri 10am–3pm, Sat–Sun 10am–5pm). The **Museum of Vancouver** (Tue–Sun 10am–5pm, Thur until 8pm) is devot-

Futuristic sculpture outside the HR Macmillan Space Centre

ed to local history and anthropology. The **Vancouver Maritime Museum** (mid-May–Aug daily 10am–5pm, Sept–mid-May Tue–Sat 10am–5pm, Sun noon–5pm) traces the history of the Pacific port. Its showpiece is the *Saint-Roch*. The ship of the Royal Canadian Mounted Police sailed around the North American continent via the Panama Canal and Arctic Ocean, to plot a definitive Northwest Passage and hunt German U-boats on the way.

The area where English Bay narrows into False Creek epitomises Vancouver's taste for the good life. The once-miserable wasteland of run-down warehouses, lumber-mills, factories and railyards has been reclaimed both for the upbeat commercial enterprises that are now a familiar feature of any Canadian city with a waterfront, and as an elegant residential neighbourhood.

On **Granville Island** (in fact a triangular peninsula of land-fill), under a bridge of the same name, is a cheerful collection of markets, cafés, galleries, boutiques and theatres. Children love it not just for the toys in the Kids Market (daily 10am–6pm) but also for Granville Island Water Park, with its water slides.

False Creek has given its name to a neighbourhood of architecturally inventive houses set around garden-courtyards and terraces. The east end of the 'creek' was the site of Expo '86, perpetuated by the giant geodesic dome of **Expo Centre**. It now operates as **Science World** (Mon–Fri 10am–5pm, Sat–Sun 10am–6pm), a hands-on science centre, with everything from a dill pickle light bulb to the interior of a beaver lodge – plus a giant-screen IMAX movie theatre.

Squamish Highway

The drive over Lion's Gate Bridge to Vancouver's **North Shore** suburbs along Marine Drive and the Upper Levels Highway (Highway 99) makes a gentle introduction to your

'Timber!'

Today's lumberjack ain't what he used to be. In the good old days, he hiked his way out to British Columbia's endless wilderness to hole up for six months at a time in isolated lumber camps in a gloomy, windowless log cabin, emerging only to chop down everything in sight, stripping whole forests bare. 'Cut and run', it was called. He shaved using his axe as a razor, ate salt pork and beans for lunch and beans and salt pork for dinner. Women were barred from camp, because otherwise a lumberjack might easily get distracted and chop off a finger.

Nowadays he commutes to the forest by vehicle and uses a chain saw to fell his quota of trees, working under the direction of forestry scientists who have selected the trees on the basis of computer-generated surveys. Then, at nightfall, he drives home to his house in the suburbs. Difficult to shave with a chain saw!

exploration of the Pacific coast and its interior. The houses, elegant or rustic, are set in a microcosm of the typical British Columbian landscape, with the occasional mountain stream rushing between boulders, tall Douglas firs and red cedars, and the ocean.

Highway 99 forks towards the north, at **Horseshoe Bay** (the landing area for the ferry from Nanaimo on Vancouver Island), to become the Sea to Sky Highway for a spectacular 100km (62-mile) drive up to Whistler Mountain. The

Squamish lumberjack statue

Coastal Mountains come right down to the water's edge of the narrow **Howe Sound**, in places forming little archipelagos in the sea. Stop off at **Shannon Falls**, a short walk away from the road on an easy gravel path over footbridges into the forest. You can picnic at the bottom of the cliff and the cascade. The town of **Squamish**, known for its stunning location between the sea and the mountains, makes a useful base from which to go hiking in Garibaldi Provincial Park.

As an alternative to driving, you could travel aboard the **Rocky Mountaineer** (formerly known as the Whistler Mountaineer), taking a three-hour train journey from Vancouver to Whistler that follows the Sea to Sky Highway. The first part of the route follows along the shores of Howe Sound, offering lovely views of the Coastal Mountains. At the top of the Sound it heads north and inland towards Whistler, taking in Shannon Falls, Mount Garibaldi, the spectacular Cheakamus Canyon, past Brandywine Falls, before finally reaching Whistler.

It's certainly a relaxing way to view the cascading waterfalls, old-growth forests, snow-capped mountain peaks and sparkling Pacific waters. The train departs from North Vancouver but you will be transported between downtown Vancouver and the station by motor coach.

Whistler Valley, only two hours' drive north of Vancouver, is spangled with lakes fed by glaciers. The road there is justly considered one of the most beautiful in the world. At the winter-sports resort of Whistler, 100km (62 miles north of Vancouver) more than 2,862 hectares (6,924 acres) of skiing territory await you. The two mountains of Whistler and Blackcomb, which reach an altitude of more than 1,600m (5,250ft), have the longest skiing season in Canada – it lasts until August. Once you're at the top there are 200 or so marked trails to choose from. And when you're ready to take a breather there are a number of mountain restaurants available.

White water rafting in Whistler Valley

The only way to visit Whistler village is on foot. The village, which has all the facilities you would expect given its proximity to a big urban area, has been tastefully developed. You'll find cafés, spas, galleries, fashionable boutiques, night clubs, bistros, restaurants that offer gastronomic menus, and much else besides.

In summer, Whistler offers excellent facilities for cycling, kayaking, river-rafting and hiking, or more sedate swimming, golf and tennis. Within just 20 minutes you can reach the summit of Whistler Mountain, thanks to the Whistler Gondola, one of the world's most sophisticated high-speed lift systems. From the top, admire the views across the Coastal Mountains. There are 18 hiking trails to explore from here. But beware of a pretty yellow flower known as skunk cabbage: when you pick it, it unleashes a smell worthy of its name.

As a co-host (with Vancouver) of the 2010 Winter Olympic Games, Whistler already offered a host of year-round activities. The **Adventure Zone** entertains the family with rides such as the Westcoaster Luge, a 1.4km (¾-mile) joyride down the lower part of the mountain, horseback riding and a wall-climbing centre. For serious enthusiasts, a mountain bike park offers more than 200km (124 miles) of thrilling, lift-serviced mountain descents, while a 30km (18-mile) trail through the entire Whistler Valley is just the thing for in-line skating and regular biking. You can even, weather permitting, ski and snowboard on Blackcomb Mountain's Horstman Glacier in summer.

Victoria

The emergence of **Victoria** as a cool place to visit has been endorsed time and again over the past decade by the readers of both *Travel & Leisure* and Condé Nast's *Traveller* magazines, who have found it one of the top cities to visit in the Americas.

Situated in a sheltered spot on the southeast point of Vancouver Island, the city has flowers growing everywhere: geraniums in hanging baskets in the shopping streets; hydrangeas and roses in the lovingly tended private gardens; shrubs and more exotic blooms in the city's parks and conservatories.

In February, while the rest of Canada is still shivering, just across the Strait of Georgia the people of Victoria are out in their parks and gardens for the annual flower-count. This tongue-in-cheek count racked up over 260 million in 2011. For Victoria is blessed with an exceptionally mild climate, with enough rain to water the flowers, and an annual average of 2,183 hours of sun to give them their brilliant colours.

Looking across Victoria's Inner Harbour

The city is also rich in cultural entertainment, from live theatre performances to art shows, concerts ranging from blues to rock, classical to jazz, summer festivals and films. In recent years, Victoria has become a gourmet getaway, offering West Coast cuisine based on the freshest local ingredients that reflect the wild Pacific Northwest. Seafood, in particular salmon and shellfish, is a mainstay of West Coast cuisine and can be caught fresh from Pacific waters. In addition, Vancouver Island wineries complete the gourmet experience by providing excellent locally made wine.

The port is more pleasure- than work-oriented, filling its harbours with cruise liners and yachts, ferries and seaplanes. Parliament reminds one and all of the town's venerable past and more serious role as British Columbia's legislative capital, and nothing prevents the sacrosanct ritual of taking tea, a symbolic act of allegiance to Britain and one that underlines Victoria's leisurely pace of life. The town is small enough to get around on foot, but there are also horse-drawn carriages and red double-decker buses modelled on London's.

The **Parliament Buildings** (mid–May–early Sept Mon–Thur 9am–5pm, Fri–Sun 9am–6pm, early Sept–early May Mon–Fri 9am–5pm) reinforces the impression that Victoria is a toy-town. Built in 1897, it was erected by someone with a playful sense of what might best evoke merry old England. There's a bit of London's St Paul's Cathedral in the huge central dome topped, for want of a saint, by a gilded statue of Captain George Vancouver. The neo-Romanesque arched entrance recalls London's Natural Science Museum, and the smaller-domed turrets suggest an Englishman's castle. The fairytale effect is enhanced at night when thousands of light bulbs outline the building.

In the **rotunda** of the dome, George Southwell has painted allegories of the four virtues that 'made' British Columbia: *Courage*, as shown by George Vancouver confronting the Spanish at Nootka Sound in 1792; *Spirit of Enterprise,* with James Douglas establishing Fort Victoria for the Hudson's Bay Company in 1842; *Work*, by those who had to build the Fort; and *Justice*, meted out to the unruly mob engaged in the 1858 gold rush. A bronze statue of Queen Victoria stands in the Parliament grounds. It was she who chose the name of British Columbia – over New Caledonia, New Hanover, New Cornwall or New Georgia.

Located immediately east of the Parliament, the **Royal BC Museum** (daily 10am–5pm, early June–late Sept Fri–Sat until 10pm) is devoted to British Columbia's fauna and flora as well as a first-rate collection of BC's First Nations' art in the First Peoples Gallery. In front of the museum stands the 62-bell **Netherlands Carillon Tower**, a gift from BC's Dutch community and the tallest bell-tower in the country.

Parliament Buildings by night

Further east is **Thunderbird Park**, home of the city's most important collection of First Nations' carvings: Tsimshian and Haida totem poles, sculptures of Salish chieftains, and a Kwakwaka'wakw house. The thunderbird, a mythical creature whose eyes flashed the lightning and whose beating wings rumbled the thunder, features in many of the carvings. In a workshop, First Nations still practise the ancient skills, but with modern tools. Most of the park's carvings date from the last half of the 19th century, but are restored and replaced when the elements get the better of them.

Just north of here, the **Fairmont Empress** is so renowned for its elegant teas that it schedules four afternoon sittings (reservations necessary). The Empress opened in 1908 to serve passengers ferried across from the western terminus of the Canadian

The Scandalous Mr Rattenbury

Francis Mawson Rattenbury left England for Victoria in 1892, aged 25. He designed some of the city's most famous structures, including the Parliament Buildings, the Empress Hotel and the Crystal Gardens. The young, brash architect assured his reputation when he won the competition to design the Parliament Building. 'Ratz', as he was known, later designed private and public buildings throughout the province.

Whether success went to his head, or he succumbed to a mid-life crisis, the second half of his life didn't go as smoothly as the first. In his mid-50s, the much celebrated Rattenbury left his wife for a younger woman. This liaison with Alma Packenham shocked the prudish Victorian society, which snubbed the couple.

So they returned to England, where Alma took up with their 18-year-old chauffeur, George Stoner. In 1935, fearing that Rattenbury knew of their affair, Stoner clubbed the 68-year-old architect to death as he slept in an armchair. Alma committed suicide days after she was acquitted of murder, and Stoner, who had been sentenced to hang, was eventually released from prison.

Pacific and is the archetypal grand old railway hotel.

The **Inner Harbour** is a pleasant place to wander among the yachts and sea-planes. The harbour's **Pacific Undersea Gardens** (daily Sept–Apr 10am–4pm, Sat–Sun until 5pm, May–June 10am–5pm, Thur–Sun until 7pm, July–Sept 9am–8pm) is an un-usually well-presented natural aquarium that visitors can view from galleries 5m (15 ft) beneath the sea.

Happy to be in Victoria

In addition to its fine models of ships, the **Maritime Museum of British Columbia** (Bastion Square; daily 10am–5pm) contains navigational paraphernalia of the old merchant ships – whalers, steamers and old Hudson's Bay paddle-wheelers. The star attraction is the original Tilikum, a 11.5m (38ft) dugout canoe equipped with three sails to take Captain J.C. Voss on an incredible three-year voyage round the world beginning in 1901. He sailed from Victoria via Australia, New Zealand, Brazil, the Cape of Good Hope and the Azores and landed up in the English town of Margate.

At the corner of Dallas Road and Douglas Street is Kilometer Zero of the 7,821km (4,860-mile) Trans-Canada Highway (which ends up, with the aid of a ferry or two, in St John's, Newfoundland). An apotheosis of flowers and greenery, **Beacon Hill Park** is an expanse of gently rolling flower-bordered lawns and groves of cedar and oak sloping down to the Pacific Ocean. Look for the 39m (128ft) totem pole carved by Chief Mungo Martin and believed to be the tallest free-standing pole cut from one tree.

Reached via a short ferry ride from in front of the Fairmont Empress (or by car), **Point Ellice House** (May–Sept 11am–4pm)

Butchart Gardens – a floral paradise

overlooks Victoria's scenic Gorge Waterway and features western Canada's finest collection of Victoriana in its original setting. Built in the 1850s, the rambling Italianate house belonged to one family for over a century, until it became a provincial historic site in 1974. Visitors come as much for its high-tea service as for its antiques and lovely gardens.

The Italianate **Emily Carr House** (207 Government Street; May–Sept Tue–Sat 11am–4pm) contains works by BC's best-known female artist *(see page 158)* as well as memorabilia, rotating exhibitions and a personal glimpse of Emily's childhood home. The **Art Gallery of Greater Victoria** (1040 Moss Street; daily 10am–5pm, Thur until 9pm, Sun noon–5pm) has a permanent exhibition of paintings by Emily Carr along with works by other Canadian, and some Asian, artists.

Drive 22km (13 miles) north of town to **Butchart Gardens** (daily mid-June–Aug 9am–10pm, closes earlier at other times of year), a century-old world-renowned quarry garden. Robert Pim Butchart made a fortune out of Portland cement at the start of the 20th century and was left with an exhausted limestone quarry. His wife suggested turning it into a garden. The result is a bewilderingly beautiful 22-hectare (55-acre) garden of fountains, lakes, rock gardens, trees and flowers. It includes the **Sunken Garden**, with symmetrical Trees of Life and a rockery of gentian, saxifrage, and Lebanon candytuft; the **Rose Garden**, at its best in July, containing 150 varieties of hybrid tea and floribunda roses; the **Japanese Garden**, with scarlet azaleas, Himalayan blue poppies, weeping larch and, by the pond, a couple of cranes to bring you good luck; and finally the dreamy **Italian Garden**, where cypresses evoke Tuscany around a water lily-filled cruciform basin (formerly the Butcharts' tennis court). The gardens are regularly used as a setting for firework shows as well as numerous theatre productions during the summer.

Vancouver Island

The mountainous island, 450km (280 miles) long and averaging 80km (48 miles) wide, is heavily forested, with some of the world's largest spruce trees, measuring up to 95m (312ft) high. This is a boon to one of the province's most important industries, but also a magnet for nature-lovers, who hike or flyfish for trout in the interior and then make for the superb sandy beaches along the island's west coast, to picnic or troll for Pacific salmon. For several thousand years, **Vancouver Island** has been a favoured spot for First Nations hunters and fishermen living around the sheltered coves and fjords that penetrate deep inland.

From Vancouver, board the car ferry either at Horseshoe Bay or Tsawwassen for Nanaimo and head north on Highway 19. Turn west at Parksville to cross the island on Highway 4, through fine forestland: the red cedar used for indigenous people's canoes, totem poles and longhouses; stately Douglas fir, mainstay of colonisers' bridges, boats, houses and flagstaffs; and Sitka spruce, the local Christmas tree.

About 20km (12 miles) from Parksville, look out for a signpost to **Little Qualicum Falls**. The well-marked walk loops around the upper falls tumbling into a ravine, then follows the river rapids to the lower falls that crash into another rocky gorge. Driving on for a few kilometres, you come to **Cameron Lake**, where you can go for a swim or have a picnic.

Highway 4 follows the lakeshore to **Cathedral Grove**, a formidable stand of Douglas firs in MacMillan Provincial Park. Many of the firs, up to 76m (250ft) high, are more than 300 years old, the most ancient dating back to the 12th century. Excellent explanatory panels trace the phases of the trees' growth. Wandering along the trails, it is easy to lose yourself in the atmosphere of a truly primeval forest.

21 ► Stock up on picnic supplies in Port Alberni and continue past Kennedy Lake to **Pacific Rim National Park Reserve**. Its sandy beaches are a delight, and the powerful ocean-breakers are admired by champion surfers. At the coast, Highway 4 turns north along one of the best resort areas, the self-explanatory **Long Beach**, 12km (7½ miles) of fine sand and first-class surfing, all year round. Hotels here provide you with cooking facilities for whatever fish you – or a generous neighbour – might catch.

Long Beach: fine sand and surf

The boardwalk that rambles along **Wickaninnish Bay** will take you in and out of the coastal pine forest. **Florencia Bay** is a good bathing beach, while **South Bay** is the mecca for collectors of 'worry stones'. Enthusiasts gather these exquisite green, aubergine or (most prized of all) jet black pebbles from hidden crannies and sort them for size, shape and texture until the ideal stone is found – a highly subjective appraisal. All others are discarded and the collector can be seen caressing the pebble, smoothing all worries away. From **Comber's Beach**, you can spot sea lions on the rocks, basking in the sun.

The peaceful fishing village of **Tofino** is home to a community of ecologists, painters and poets whose independent way of life in harmony with nature contrasts with that of the rest of British Columbia. The **Eagle Aerie Gallery** (daily 10am–5pm), in a traditional longhouse, displays the work of its artist-owner, Roy Henry Wickers.

On the northeast coast of the island, the coastal **Cape Scott Province Park** offers a host of outdoor challenges and is popular with kayakers and canoeists. Departing from Port Hardy, BC Ferries organises a daytime or overnight cruise through the spectacular **Inside Passage**, between the densely forested island coast and the nordic fjords of the mainland.

Fraser and Thompson Canyons

This stark mountain landscape of pine forest, progressively thinning out to more arid, craggy canyons above the fast-flowing river, is the pioneer country that made British Columbia.

Driving east from Vancouver on the Trans-Canada Highway and following the Fraser River north to its tributary, the Thompson, you are backtracking along the great exploration route traced by intrepid fur traders from the prairies to the Pacific. It is also the route unerringly followed by millions of Pacific salmon between the ocean and their spawning grounds far inland. And, against all the odds of the terrain, it's the route the railway builders chose to carry the riches of lumber and mining – and the first tourists – across the continent.

The old rivalry between the two railway companies, Canadian Pacific and Canadian National, becomes particularly evident when endless trains of freight wagons, often attached to two powerful locomotives for the tougher stretches, snake through the canyons on opposite banks of the river.

Turn north at **Hope** to **Yale**, an old fort of the Hudson's Bay Company, terminus of its stern-wheelers that were unable to negotiate the rapids upriver. At low water you can still see the ring tie-ups they used on the river bank. The small **museum** (daily May–Sept 10am–5pm) tells the story of how this village of only a few hundred people was once a gold rush boomtown and the major construction depot for the Canadian Pacific Railway.

The strands of British Columbia's destiny come together where the Fraser Canyon narrows at the torrential rapids of **Hell's Gate**. For thousands of years, this point in the river's descent to the ocean was the First Nations' favoured fishing spot to catch the salmon swimming to their spawning grounds. It was here, in 1808, that they helped Nor'wester fur trader Simon Fraser get

A Salmon Primer

Of the five species of Canada's Pacific salmon – sockeye, pink, coho, chum and chinook – the sockeye is the most appreciated for its food value. Caught before spawning, it is bright red, rich in oil, and retains its colour and flavour in processing.

It spawns in tributary streams above a lake. The hatched young makes its way down to the lake to grow on a diet of water fleas to a length of 7.5 to 10cm (3 to 4in). After one or two years, it's time for the ocean, a journey of up to 1,600km (1,000 miles). After three summers at sea, feeding off shrimp, the salmon (weighing 1.8kg–2.6kg/4–6lb) returns in autumn to spawn in its native river. Battering its way upstream and leaping obstacles, the salmon instinctively seeks out the original stream where it began as an egg four years earlier. At the spawning ground, the female scours a nest or 'redd' with her tail and deposits some 3,500 pink-red eggs. The male, which has grown a hump and fierce hooked snout to fight off rivals during the mating period, sprays the eggs with his sperm. Within 10 days the adults die. The following spring, the new cycle begins.

his canoe past the rapids, then over a swaying ropeway of vines strung along the canyon wall, enabling him to follow to the ocean the river that now bears his name.

In 1913, the Canadian National blocked the salmon's passage with rock-blasts through the canyon to build the railway. The consequent 90 percent reduction of the annual sockeye salmon catch was remedied only 30 years later when multimillion-dollar steel-and-concrete channels were built for the fish.

Hell's Gate

First Nations people fish here again nowadays, but their modest catch can't compete with the millions caught by the commercial fisheries at the Fraser estuary. Take the **cable car** across the gorge for a close-up view of the rapids. At the restaurant by the cable-car terminal, try a grilled salmon lunch for a taste of what the fuss is all about.

The Thompson River joins the Fraser at **Lytton**. Before turning east on the Trans-Canada Highway to follow the Thompson, make a detour just north of town (on Highway 12) to see the dramatic effect of the **confluence** mixing the lime of the tributary with the clearer mountain waters of the Fraser.

The drier Thompson valley soon takes on a more rugged aspect than that of the Fraser, with the sagebrush and bighorn sheep of a semi-desert, in places as beautifully desolate as a moonscape. The similarity with America's southwest is reinforced by the ranches that you can see around **Kamloops Lake**.

If you are here in October, you may see the spectacular **salmon run**, when the waters turn scarlet with thousands of sockeye. On the Trans-Canada Highway, take the turn-off at Squilax Bridge to the junction of the Adams River and Shuswap Lake. On the Thompson River, summer visitors can try the bumpy thrills of the sockeye experience for themselves with some whitewater river rafting organised out of Vancouver. Ask at the city tourist information office for details.

Okanagan Valley

Before heading east to the Rocky Mountains, turn south on Highway 97 to the lovely **Okanagan Valley** (about four hours east of Vancouver) for golf, tennis, swimming, hiking, camping, and fishing amid vineyards, orchards (this is Canada's best-known fruit belt), and dozens of trout lakes. The Okanagan River widens into an elongated lake with excellent sandy beaches, sailing, and other water sports facilities based on **Kelowna**, the hub or the Okanagan fruit belt.

Across the lake at **Westbank**, among other orchard towns, you pay for what you pick: apricots, peaches, cherries, plums, pears and apples all grow here. At the southern end of the lake, the resort town of Penticton stages a Peach Festival in August.

Sunny Okanagan Valley is one of the main wine-producing areas in Canada (the other being Ontario's Niagara Peninsula). More than 65 wineries propose tastings and sales of their pleasing dry whites and dry reds along with some more refined wines from the nobler European varieties: Pinot Noir, Cabernet Sauvignon, Chardonnay, Gewürztraminer and Riesling. Among the wineries you can visit are Calona and Cedar Creek in Kelowna, Mission Hill in Westbank and Gray Monk at **Okanagan Centre**.

THE ROCKIES AND COLUMBIA MOUNTAINS

The national parks of Canada's **Rocky Mountains** provide unrivalled opportunities for exhilarating contacts with a wilderness where you can go camping, hiking through the forests, fishing in the lakes and rivers, or canoeing and whitewater rafting in the

Grand panorama of the Rockies

mountain torrents. And skiing, downhill and cross-country, were greatly enhanced by the facilities installed for Calgary's 1988 Winter Olympics. If there's one region that merits all the superlatives, this is it. The Rockies should form part of the programme for all visitors to western Canada, whether they are hikers, skiers, mountaineers or loafers simply seeking to relax in a hot springs spa or beside a cool, sparkling lake.

The Canadian part of North America's most important mountain chain, which stretches from the Yukon Territory to the Mexican frontier, straddles the border of British Columbia and Alberta. The Canadian Rockies are divided into the superbly administered national parks of Kootenay, Yoho, Banff and Jasper, whilst the nearby Mount Revelstoke and Glacier national parks form part of the Columbia Mountains. Be aware that most of the parks charge an entrance fee, and park-rangers carry out permit checks. You can either buy a one-day permit, or invest in an annual permit that admits a vehicle and up to seven occupants to more than 100 participating national parks.

The parks protect the fauna

The stark landscapes testify to the relative youth, in geological terms, of the Rockies. Sedimentary rock lifted by thrust faults 60 million years ago has resulted in the creation of striking silhouettes in the shape of fortress battlements, sawteeth or single pyramids like the Matterhorn. The highest peak in the Canadian Rockies is Mount Robson, 3,954m (12,972ft), just inside British Columbia.

Mount Revelstoke

The road through the Monashee mountains to **Mount Revelstoke National Park** follows the Eagle River and the route of the Canadian Pacific Railway on the crucial stretch that enabled the railway to break through the Rockies. At Craigellachie, right beside the road, about 25km (15 miles) east of Shuswap Lake, a stone cairn marks the spot where the eastern and western sections linked up to form Canada's first transcontinental railway. At 9.22am on 7 November 1885, surrounded by top-hatted dignitaries, the CPR boss Donald Smith hammered home the famous Last Spike(he bent the first spike with a misjudged swing).

Leave the Trans-Canada Highway 1.5km (1 mile) east of the city of Revelstoke to drive the winding **Meadows in the Sky Parkway** (only open during the snow-free season) up Mount Revelstoke (1,920m/6,299ft), one of the few mountains in Canada with a summit accessible by vehicle (a shuttle bus transfers you from the parking area to the top). This is a comfortable way to watch the park's landscape change from dense lowland forest, through alpine meadows dotted with wild flowers, to the bleak tundra of the high country. From the top you look out over the Beaver and Illecillewaet river valleys and over to the Monashee and Selkirk mountains.

There are no vehicle-accessible camp sites inside the park, only designated backcountry campsites. If you plan to camp overnight along the 65km (40 miles) of trails, check in with the park office in downtown Revelstoke (PO Box 350, Revelstoke, BC VOE2SO; tel: 250-837 7500), who provide detailed maps.

It is not unusual to see mountain goats and the occasional moose, or difficult to spot grey jay and bald eagle. Be on the lookout for black bears.

The Trans-Canada continues through the jagged mountains of **Glacier National Park**, which contains more than 400 glaciers. **Rogers Pass** was named after the major who found this corridor

Parks – National and Provincial

To make the wilderness accessible without spoiling its beauty, Canada has created 42 national parks (along with four marine conservation areas). They come in all sorts and sizes, and range from the little bird sanctuary of Point Pelee at the southernmost tip of Ontario to the gigantic Wood Buffalo park (bigger than Switzerland) that straddles Alberta and the Northwest Territories. They encompass the beaches of Vancouver Island's Pacific Rim and the primeval ice of Auyuittuq on Baffin Island. These 42 national parks are supplemented by close to 2,000 provincial parks run by local governments.

Park regulations are simple but strict. For example, it is forbidden to pick flowers or cut down trees for wood; hunting on park grounds is prohibited except where explicitly authorised, and fishing is permitted only with a licence; no motorboats are allowed except where explicitly authorised. You should always stop by the park reception centre to pick up maps, a fishing licence, advice about camp sites, and possibly a guide for nature tours or fishing expeditions.

the crowds and get a great view of the hotel in its surroundings, walk to the far end of the lake along the marked path.

Another option is to take the mountain road 14km (8½ miles) south to **Moraine Lake** – a nice drive, or a wonderful all-day hike – to view the sawtooth skyline of the **Valley of the Ten Peaks**. The valley overlooks Moraine Lake and its magical, clear, turquoise waters. For a spectacular view of the whole area, take the gondola ride from Lake Louise to **Mount Whitehorn**.

Banff National Park

The history of the first and most famous of Canada's national parks began with the railways. When the Canadian Pacific reached Banff in 1883, the Rockies were suddenly opened up to public access. Railway workers discovered hot sulphur springs, and the federal government, conscious of the huge economic and tourist potential of the discovery and the need to protect the hot springs, bought the rights to the concession and created a nat-

Banff National Park

ural reserve. Two years later the government decided to preserve the beauty of the region by protecting it as **Banff National Park**.

In 1886, in the Valley of the River Bow, the Canadian Pacific built one of their grandest castle-hotels, the **Fairmont Banff Springs Hotel**, reminiscent of the fairytale castles of Ludwig II of Bavaria. Go out on a canoe on the river, or, if you're feeling less energetic, visit the **Cave and Basin National Historic Site**, 3km (2 miles) west of the hotel, or take a dip at **Upper Hot Springs**, a short drive south. The temperature of the spring water feeding the outdoor pool is 47°C (116°F) in winter, dropping to 27°C (81°F) in summer. The eight-minute gondola ride from Upper Hot Springs up **Sulphur Mountain** (2,500m/8,200ft) will give you a panoramic view of the mountains around the Bow Valley.

One of many fine excursions is the drive along Bow Valley Parkway (Highway 1A), then a hike along the marked trail beside the rapids to the lower and upper waterfalls in **Johnston Canyon**. Back on the Trans-Canada Highway towards Lake Louise, look to the east for **Castle Mountain**, 3,000m (9,840ft) high.

Icefields Parkway

Icefields Parkway, the 230km (142-mile) drive on Highway 93 up the spine of the mountain range between Lake Louise and Jasper allows you to discover the incredible variety and beauty of the Rockies – glaciers, waterfalls, lakes and canyons. Allow at least a full day so that you have time to explore some of the sights on foot. Stop first at the **Crowfoot Glacier**, where you can see the glacier's two remaining 'toes', the third having broken away. The mass of ice facing you is 55m (180ft) thick. At Bow Summit, the highest point of the Icefields Parkway, at 2,088m (6,850ft), leave the Parkway at the signpost to the viewpoint overlooking **Peyto Lake**, a deep turquoise at the height of summer. If you have time, stop at Kilometer 119 on the Parkway, to hike up the winding path to **Parker's Ridge** (2,185m/7,165ft) above pretty alpine meadows overlooking the Saskatchewan Glacier, the start of the great North Saskatchewan River that ends up in Hudson Bay.

Horse riding in Jasper

Inside **Jasper National Park**, put on sturdy rubber- or crepe-soled shoes to walk out on to the ice of **Athabasca Glacier**, part of the Columbia Icefield. You can also venture on to the ice sheet in a 56-passenger Ice Explorer bus. Notice the frontal moraine (the rock debris or rubble that the glacier pushes ahead of itself): its location shows that the glacier is retreating. A hundred years ago it reached to the other side of the Parkway. At the Parkway's Kilometre 200 mark, take Highway 93A to **Athabasca Falls**. A boardwalk leads you on a nature walk up to where the mighty river plunges over the narrow gorge.

Jasper is a lively resort town, popular for its canoeing, kayaking, hiking, golfing, fishing and horseback riding. Its accommodations range from cosy cabins to the legendary **Fairmont Jasper Park Lodge**. Take the Jasper Tramway ride up **Whistlers Mountain** for a view of the Rockies' highest peak, Mount Robson.

One of the most attractive excursions is the drive along **Maligne Canyon**. Take time to look down into the sheer limestone gorge at the rolling waters, sudden cascades and tranquil pools. At the end of the canyon is **Maligne Lake**, where you can take a boat cruise around the much-photographed, picturesque Spirit Island.

THE PRAIRIES

Alberta, Saskatchewan and Manitoba, the three provinces of the **Prairies**, share the same rugged climate. The vast wheat fields reaching to the horizon give full meaning to the expression 'Canada's wide open spaces'. The sky, too, is spectacular, with magnificent dawns and dazzling sunsets.

The monuments and museums of Edmonton, Regina and Winnipeg, the provincial capitals, tell the history of the struggle of the Métis, buffalo-hunting descendants of native people, and the French fur traders against the invasion of English-speaking farmers from Ontario, and then against the influx of Eastern European immigrants brought in to exploit the grain wealth of the prairies.

In Manitoba, if you go up to Churchill on Hudson Bay, you will be at the heart of the fur trading companies' northern activities. If you're here in the autumn you may be fortunate enough to see a polar bear, although they very rarely venture so far south.

Alberta

Rounding up the herd

A province of ranches and oil derricks, **Alberta** cultivates the image of Canada's Wild West. If its politics are often conservative (opponents compare some of the leaders with the province's collection of dinosaurs), its people are adventurous, supporting Calgary's rodeos and Edmonton's commercial extravaganza of a vast shopping mall.

With the discovery of oil after World War II, Alberta's economy boomed, the population soared, and confidence was boosted. Today the mood remains buoyant, despite occasional down turns in oil prices.

Between 600 and 200 million years ago, the region of Alberta, alternating between dry land and sea, developed plant and animal life that decayed to form the oil, coal and natural gas at the base of the province's modern prosperity. Subsequent floods and earthquakes left the parched Badlands of the Red Deer River Valley as a protective crust, in which surveyors looking for coal seams discovered the skeletons of dinosaurs.

Calgary

In this part of the world, in past eras, gold rushes created cities out of a wasteland overnight and just as quickly returned them to dust. The oil crisis of the 1970s could have had the same effect on **Calgary,** but its shining skyscrapers do not look as if they are about to crumble. At the time the post-World War II oil boom began, Calgary was little more than a village, better known for bronco-busting rodeos than business acumen. Its population more than doubled from 280,000 in 1961 to 590,000 20 years later – almost that of the provincial capital, Edmonton, its rival. The Calgary region now has a population of more than 1.2 million. Suburbs sprawl in all directions, and the city keeps boosting civic pride with public structures such as the $75-million **Epcor Centre for the Performing Arts**, home of the Calgary Philharmonic.

Hotshot bankers have moved in to handle the new wealth, polishing up but not eclipsing the frontier image. While hand-tooled cowboy boots and Stetson hats are still popular, business suits are increasingly sophisticated, even Italian in cut, leaving the string ties and blue jeans for the annual Stampede.

The **Calgary Stampede** lasts for 10 days in early July. It is an event not to be missed, both from an anthropological point of view and for the pleasure of the spectacle. Cowboys insist on calling it the 'Greatest Outdoor Show on Earth', a title dating back to its beginnings in 1912. The Stampede was originally conceived to demonstrate the techniques of rounding up cattle on the prairies. Nowadays, at Stampede Park, there are agricultural and garden exhibitions, displays of Native crafts and dancing, and all

Native American Indian mosaic at the Glenbow Museum

the sideshows of a country fair. But after the opening **parade** of
baton-twirling majorettes, floats, cowboys, costumed Natives and
champion steers, the big attraction remains the **rodeo**. Spectators watch bareback-riding and bronco-busting, bull-riding and
steer-wrestling, calf-roping and Indian buffalo-riding and, above
all, traditional **chuckwagon races**. In the Rangeland Derby, as
it is known, the wagons, drawn by four horses, are identical to
those used to bring food out to the cowboys on the range at
roundup time. According to popular belief, the origin of the
Derby dates from the time when the last crew back in town had
to buy all the drinks; nowadays the prize money totals more than
$550,000.

In downtown Calgary, take time to visit the **Glenbow Museum** (130 Ninth Avenue SE; Mon–Sat 9am–5pm, Sun noon–5pm).
Beautifully arranged exhibits of furniture, costumes, utensils and
weapons give a vivid picture of Alberta life, from the pioneers'
log-cabin homesteads to oil-drillers, railway-builders and miners.

The downtown skyscrapers are linked by a network of bridges

and subterranean galleries. One of the main shopping centres is the four-block **Stephen Avenue Mall**, a civilised thoroughfare of two-storey buildings and street-level shops with benches and musicians to provide entertainment. For great views of the town's steel-and-glass urban canyons and the Rocky Mountains looming on the western horizon, take the lift to the observation deck of the 191m (627ft) **Calgary Tower** (daily June–Aug 9am–10pm, Sept–May 9am–9pm).

The 17,000-seat **Saddledome**, created for the 1988 Olympics at Stampede Park, is equipped for ice hockey and figure skating. A speed-skating rink has been installed in the **Olympic Oval** on the University of Calgary campus. On Bowfort Road, the **Canada Olympic Park** features three ski-jumps and a combined bobsleigh and luge run.

Dog sledding in Kananaskis Country

A 50-minute drive west of Calgary brings you to **Kananaskis Country**. People come to hike, bike, fish or go horseback riding; cross-country skiing, downhill skiing, snow shoeing and dog sledding at Nakiska ski resort are popular in winter. **Canmore** (1½ hours west of Calgary) sits in a virtual cape of the Canadian Rockies. Bordered by Banff National Park and Kananaskis Country, it's another excellent base for outdoor adventuring.

Prehistoric Finds

The **Alberta Badlands**, once part of a subtropical swamp that sheltered a vast array of prehistoric life, contain one of the world's finest repositories of dinosaur fossils. The most spectacular badlands are preserved along the Red Deer River in Unesco World Heritage Site **Dinosaur Provincial Park**, 175km (108 miles) east of Calgary. From a lookout

Can you feel it?

Can You Feel It? was the theme song for the 1988 Calgary Winter Olympics, and it reflects this dynamic city that some say feels nothing like the rest of Canada.

near the entrance you can survey 7,000 hectares (17,300 acres) of this gnarled, sandstone landscape with its weirdly eroded formation. A circular 5km (3-mile) drive with side trips on foot leads to dinosaur bones preserved where they were found. Open year round for camping, hiking or cross-country skiing – depending upon the season – other areas of the park are accessible on organised tours and hikes (May–Oct; reservations tel: 403-378 4344).

The town of **Drumheller**, 138km (86 miles) northeast of Calgary, lies deep within the badlands, which drop abruptly here below the lip of the prairie. From Calgary, head north towards the **Canadian Badlands Trail** on Highway 2 to Crossfield and then east on Highway 72 (which becomes Highway 9). Make a point of stopping off at **Horseshoe Canyon**, a picturesque pocket of badlands amidst the prairies. Continue along Highway 9 to Drumheller where the **Dinosaur Trail** begins. Before you venture out on this scenic loop through Alberta's lunar-like badlands, check out the murals of dinosaurs on the town's historic buildings, and, on the banks of the Red Deer River, the world's largest fibreglass *Tyrannosaurus rex*.

Heading out on **North Dinosaur Trail**, 6km (4 miles) west of Drumheller, is the **Royal Tyrrell Museum of Palaeontology**, arguably the finest dinosaur museum in the world (mid-May–Aug daily 9am–9pm, Sept–mid-May Tue–Sun 10am–5pm). Superbly organised and presented, the museum has a backdrop of prehistoric jungle for the 200 reconstructed skeletons and Paleistic

models, which include *Alber-
tosaurus*, the awesome *Tyrannosaurus rex*, and the 'tiny'
but lovable duck-billed *Lam-
beosaurus*, just 3m (10ft) tall,
followed by her baby.

**Head-Smashed-In Buffalo
Jump Interpretive Centre**
(daily 10am–5pm), 18km (11
miles) north-west of Fort Macleod on Highway 785, portrays
the buffalo-hunting culture of the Plains peoples from ancient
times to the arrival of the Europeans. The 'jump' was used for
at least 5,500 years and has been carefully preserved. **Crowsnest
Pass** straddles the Alberta/BC border and is one of the most
scenic routes through the Rockies. Nearby, on April 29, 1903,
82 million tonnes of limestone crashed from the summit of Turtle Mountain and buried a portion of the town of Frank. The
terrible power of nature over humankind is preserved and ex-
plained at the **Frank Slide Interpretive Centre**.

Edmonton

In the geographic heart of the province, **Edmonton** is both the
province's capital, and a cultural hotbed, renowned for its museums, historic neighbourhoods and festivals. That said, its great
crowd pleaser is **West Edmonton Mall**, with over 800 stores and
ten theme-park attractions. For a sense of the city's history, **Fort
Edmonton Park** (mid-May–June Mon–Fri 10am–4pm, Sat–Sun
10am–6pm, July–Aug daily 10am–6pm, Sept Sat–Sun only 10am–
4pm) portrays life as an early pioneer, and is Canada's largest living history park. The **Royal Alberta Museum** (daily 9am–5pm)
explores western Canada's human and natural history.

The North Saskatchewan River winds through Edmonton,
bordered by parks and woodland trails. In the heart of the valley, the four massive glass pyramids of the **Muttart Conservatory** (daily) are an indoor paradise that showcases the flora of

various climes – from a steaming jungle to a sun-baked desert.

East of Edmonton, on the Trans-Canada Yellowhead Highway 16, costumed interpreters play the role of settlers who arrived in this area between the late 1800s and the 1930s in the **Ukrainian Cultural Heritage Village** (mid-May–early Sept daily 10am–5pm). Nearby is **Elk Island National Park** (year round), home to elk, plains bison, wood bison, deer, moose and beaver.

Saskatchewan

Although revenues from oil, uranium, coal and natural gas now approach agricultural income, Saskatchewan is still known as 'Canada's bread basket'. The Depression of the 1930s plunged the province into poverty, but that all changed with the rise of local boy John Diefenbaker as the first federal prime minister from Saskatchewan. Farmers won't ever forget the deals he got for their high-grade wheat in Russia and China. You can see the monuments across the Prairies – huge, cathedral-like grain silos.

Saskatchewan players

Regina

Long before the first settlers arrived in the 1880s, and before it came the provincial capital in 1905, Regina was known as Pile O'Bones. The name stemmed from the early Plains Indian ritual of stacking buffalo bones together along the banks of Wascana Creek. They believed bison would stay in the area if it contained bones of their own kind. The First Nations continue to be a strong element in the area's culture. Saskatchewan is home to many champion Native dancers and drum groups, including in Regina. For a comprehensive understanding of their history, visit the First Nations Gallery at the **Royal Saskatchewan Museum** (2445 Albert Street; daily May–Aug 9am–5.30pm, Sept–Apr 9am–4.30pm), which traces 10,000 years of aboriginal history and depicts traditional clothing and a typical tipi encampment.

The museum is south of the city centre in **Wascana Park**, an inviting 930-hectare (2,300-acre) forest of 350,000 trees. Other attractions within the park include the **Saskatchewan Legisla-**

Saskatchewan Legislative Building

tive Building, a fine limestone edifice rising beside Wascana Lake; the **MacKenzie Art Gallery** (3475 Albert Street, Mon–Thur 10am–5.30pm, Fri until 9pm, Sat–Sun noon– 5.30pm), a showcase of contemporary and historical artworks; and the **Conexus Arts Centre**, home to the Regina Symphony Orchestra.

North of the airport, at the end of 11th Avenue, is the **Royal Canadian Mounted Police** training academy for

Regina has strong links with the Mounties

recruits. The Sunset Retreat ceremonies (July–mid-Aug Tue evenings) draw a crowd to see the RCMP Cadet Band and the troops on horseback in their traditional scarlet tunics. Located on the academy's grounds is a stunning glass and concrete building housing the **RCMP Heritage Centre** (daily 9am–6pm), which uses interactive exhibits to trace the history of the Mounties from the first clashes with gold-rush panhandlers to post-World War II counter-espionage.

A short drive east of Regina, the **Qu'Appelle Valley** is a stunning sunken garden carved out by glaciers approximately 18,000 years ago. A chain of lakes and parks, connected by the Qu'Appelle River, stretches from Buffalo Pound Provincial Park in the west to Round Lake in the east and offers plenty of opportunities for hiking, swimming, fishing and golfing.

Manitoba

The population of this province of prairies, boreal forest and lakes presents an astonishingly rich ethnic diversity. To the Anglo Saxon and French, established since the time of the fur trade, were added late 19th-century immigrants, who have

Winnipeg's business district

given Manitoba thriving communities of Ukrainian, German, Jewish, Polish, Dutch, Hungarian, Italian and even Icelandic origin, with more recent arrivals from Asia and the Philippines.

Winnipeg

Of the province's population, well over half (753,000) lives in its capital. In addition to being the seat of government administration, **Winnipeg** has a stalwart business community and a flourishing cultural life, especially in modern art, ballet and classical music. Manitoba's many ethnic cultures provide the basis for its **Folklorama** festival, which every summer attracts close to 50 pavilions featuring national cuisines, folklore, craftwork and costumes.

The town's artistic and commercial worlds joined forces to preserve and restore the handsome, early 20th-century architecture of the old business district, a 15-block area bounded by Princess and Main streets and William and Notre-Dame avenues.

The **Exchange District**, as it is now known, contains many fine office buildings and warehouses inspired by the Chicago School, including the **Royal Tower** (504 Main Street), built in 1903. During summer weekends, Old Market Square has stalls selling everything from fruit and vegetables to crafts and bric-a-brac.

In the splendid **Manitoba Museum** (190 Rupert Avenue; daily summer 10am–5pm, winter Tue–Fri 10am–4pm, Sat–Sun 11am–5pm), prehistoric and present-day animals are presented in beautifully recreated environments of Arctic wastelands, tundra, woodland and waterfalls, complete with bird sounds, wolf howls, or the terrifying roar of a forest fire. The province's ethnic groups are shown in national costume and traditional homesteads; special emphasis is given to the First Nations of Manitoba and a Métis buffalo hunt. There is also a reconstruction of the **Nonsuch**, a Hudson's Bay Company ketch that in 1669 carried the first cargo of furs from Canada to England. The museum adjoins the **Centennial Concert Hall**, home of the Winnipeg Symphony Orchestra, Manitoba Opera Association and Royal Winnipeg Ballet.

Within the strikingly designed structure of **Winnipeg Art**

Louis Riel, Rebel and Martyr

Was the founder of Manitoba a political hero or mad visionary? Few characters in Canadian history have excited more controversy than the French-Indian Métis leader, Louis Riel, born in 1844 in the Red River colony that was to become Winnipeg.

Riel studied theology and law in Montréal. He proved to be courageous and capable when he worked out feasible legislation for Manitoba's new status as a Canadian province in 1870. But his volatile personality cracked under the strains of armed conflict, American exile, and finally imprisonment for his role in the execution of Ontario agitator, Thomas Scott. In mental institutions in Québec, Riel lapsed into moral decline and lost his sense of reality. He conceived a religious mission to set up a New World Catholicism with the Bishop of Montréal as its pope. He went back into US exile, this time self-imposed, until 1884, when Métis farmers begged him to come and defend their legal rights in Saskatchewan.

His armed rebellion of 1885, centring on the Métis stronghold of Batoche, with a new 'provisional government' like the one that had forced concessions from Ottawa 15 years earlier, collapsed within two months. At his trial for treason, the jury found him guilty, but recommended clemency. Despite conflicting expert arguments on his sanity, Riel was hanged in Regina on 16 November 1885, sparking the beginning of the nationalist movement. Métis and Québécois campaign to this day for a retroactive pardon.

Gallery (300 Memorial Boulevard; Tue–Sun 11am–5pm, Thur until 9pm) is an extensive collection of works by modern Canadian and American artists and the world's largest collection of contemporary Inuit art. Seasonal exhibitions here are usually first-rate.

At the junction of the Assiniboine and Red Rivers, **The Forks**, dubbed Winnipeg's meeting place, is the site of several summer festivals. An exciting addition to the museum scene, the architecturally stunning **Canadian Museum for Human Rights**, is being constructed here.

Old St Boniface, Winnipeg's French quarter, is now a suburb on the east bank of the Red River, connected to downtown by the Esplanade Riel pedestrian bridge. On avenue Taché, the convent of the Grey Nuns is the city's oldest building (1846); it has been transformed into the **St Boniface Museum** (Mon–Fri 9.30am–4.50pm, Sat–Sun noon–4pm, mid-May–Sept Thur until 8pm). It is devoted in part to the city's French roots and the life of Louis Riel *(see box, page 199)*. Next door to the museum is Riel's simple grave in the cemetery of St-Boniface basilica, rebuilt after being damaged by fire.

Near the forks of the Red and Assiniboine rivers in St Boniface, **Fort Gibraltar** (mid-May–June Mon–Fri 10am–5pm, July–Labour Day Wed–Thur 10am–6pm, Fri–Sun noon–4pm) – a replica of a fort built by the North West Company (NWC) in 1809 – recaptures the height of the fur trade with a depiction of life at the fort in 1814.

Churchill

 The historic port of **Churchill** offers a unique opportunity (with simple but comfortable hotel accommodation) to visit Hudson Bay. You can see beluga whales in summer, polar bears in the autumn, and, on more than 300 nights a year, the *aurora borealis* or Northern Lights. The easiest way in is by plane, but if you want to see at ground level the Manitoba lakes and plains that fur traders once crossed, take the VIA train from Winnipeg for a 36-hour excursion.

The Northern Lights

The town has a true frontier atmosphere to it. The Hudson's Bay Company established a trading post here in 1717, and its store on the main street is still the place to get camping and hiking gear. In the Inuit craft shops you'll find not souvenir junk but genuine native handiwork, and leather and fur goods that do not infringe protected-species laws. The **Eskimo Museum** (June–Oct Mon 1–5pm, Tue–Sat 9am–noon and 1–5pm, Nov–May Mon–Sat 1–4.30pm) gives a good insight into the life and art of the Inuit of the Hudson Bay area.

Wildlife tours around the bay and across the otherwise inaccessible hinterland are organised in giant-wheeled or half-track tundra buggies (half-day and full-day excursions). Several **boat tours** explore the bay for close-up sightings of beluga whales in July and August and of polar bears in the fall, and cruise over to the ruins of **Fort Prince of Wales** on a promontory at the mouth of the Churchill River. In 1782, the Hudson's Bay Company's massive stone fortress surrendered to the French navigator La Pérouse without firing a single shot.

If you prefer to explore on your own, hire a car and drive around the harbour and its monumental grain silos on the way to **Cape Merry** for a good view of the fort, especially at sunset.

THE NORTH

Every country has its mythic place, and Canada's is the fabled North, the icy 'wasteland' in which the country and the world like to cloak the national image. The reality is no less fascinating. Until recently the territories situated north of 60° latitude were known only by the Inuit and First Nations who lived there, and by a few explorers and mineral prospectors.

More and more adventurers from 'the outside' are heading for the Yukon's rugged mountains and the eerily beautiful Arctic wastes of the Northwest Territories and Nunavut (the northernmost point is just 830km/515 miles from the Pole). In the old Klondike boomtowns, people find a whiff of romance from the great gold rush of 1896. Lovers of the outdoors track the last free-roaming bison herds or fly in for the challenge of fishing the trout and grayling in Great Slave and Great Bear lakes.

Access by road takes several days, but there are plenty of airlines serving the towns of **Whitehorse**, **Yellowknife** and **Iqaluit**, formerly known as Frobisher Bay (for access to the Auyuittuq National Park on Baffin Island change planes at Iqaluit for Pangnirtung).

The Yukon

The Klondike gold rush did more than fire the western world's imagination with scores of novels, epic poems and films – it opened up a whole vast territory with such mundane but essential services as railways, roads, telephones, electricity and hot and cold running water. In a sub-arctic land of mountains and glacial lakes beside the great Yukon River, today's tourists can thank yesterday's prospectors for using part of their paydirt to provide some creature comforts. Close to the original action and still providing the most vivid testimony to the Klondike days, the boomtown of **Dawson City** yielded in 1951 to the transport and communications centre of Whitehorse as territorial capital.

Whitehorse

Originally the terminus where prospectors transferred from the Skagway train to the Yukon River steamboats, **Whitehorse** rose and declined with the gold rush, and is now the junction of the Alaska and Klondike highways. The capital of the Yukon since 1953, with two-thirds of the province's population (around 26,400), this thoroughly modern town is proud of its **Old Log Church** (mid-May–Labour Day daily 10am–6pm) on Elliot Street and some old two- and three-storey log cabins that it calls 'log skyscrapers', erected when building space in town was at a premium.

Yukon gold

One of these cabins is home to the **MacBride Museum** (daily mid-May–Labour Day 9.30am–5.30pm, Labour Day– mid-May Tue–Sat 10am–4pm), with a collection of memorabilia from the gold rush days and various exhibits of Yukon wildlife.

You can visit the steamboat *SS Klondike* (daily mid-May–mid-Sept), which once plied the river to Dawson City, moored at the end of Second Avenue. Upriver, 3km (2 miles) south of town, take a two-hour **cruise** through Miles Canyon on the *MV Schwatka*.

Commissioner's Tea in all its finery, Dawson City

The **George Johnston Museum** (daily mid-May–Aug 9am–6pm), a 2¼-hour drive southeast of Whitehorse, on the Alaska Highway, offers a magnificent collection of Tlingit artefacts as well as the work of George Johnston, a Tlingit leader, trapper and renowned photographer.

Dawson City

Situated a day's drive from Whitehorse along the Klondike Highway, 240km (150 miles) south of the Arctic Circle, the gold rush boomtown of **Dawson City** counts scarcely 2,000 inhabitants today. But the body responsible for historic sites has reconstructed and restored the 'monuments' of its heyday. The history of Dawson City is further celebrated by a couple of annual events. This is the place to be mid-August, for the Klondike River raft-races, costumed street parades, music and dancing during the week-long Discovery Days Festival. If you miss it, look out for the Great Klondike International Outhouse Race at the beginning of September.

One of the town's major year-round attractions is **Diamond Tooth Gertie's Gambling Hall**, an old-fashioned (and legal) casino, where gartered dancing girls kick it up to a honky-tonk piano.

Dawson City Museum (daily mid-May–early Sept 10am–6pm) gives you all the inside information about gold-mining, displaying prospectors' tools and paraphernalia. Behind the museum is the log cabin of Robert Service, the diggers' bard celebrated for the poems *The Shooting of Dan McGrew* and *The Cremation of Sam McGee*. He himself avoided the tough life of the gold-miner for a job at the local bank. Next door is the home of Jack London, who made more money from his novels about the wild north than from the stake he worked on at nearby Henderson Creek. Both literary shrines hold readings from the masters' works.

Kluane National Park

About 150km (94 miles) west of Whitehorse on the Alaska Highway, the entrance to **Kluane National Park** is at Haines Junction. The park's St Elias Mountain Range offers a challenge to climbers, including the highest peak in Canada, the 6,050m (19,842ft) Mount Logan.

For safety reasons, check in at the park reception centre (mid-May–mid-Sept) and get maps and information on the hiking trails covering 240km (150 miles) of challenging terrain. The vast Kluane icefield system is made up of some 2,000 glaciers, and you can hike to the rim of the spectacular Kaskawulsh Glacier, visible when leaving Kluane Lake on the park's eastern edge.

Northwest Territories

If you long to see the Midnight Sun, make for these immense lands which cover 11 percent of Canada's total surface and incorporate two of the 10 largest lakes in the world: Great Slave Lake and Great Bear Lake. There, the tundra resembles lush meadowland that becomes a vibrant carpet of yellow, red and orange in the fall. In Mackenzie District, in summer, when the temperatures climb to a comfortable 21°C (70°F), there is a multicoloured explosion of wild flowers. During fall and winter (late Aug–Mar), the sky comes alive with the brilliant display of the *aurora borealis*, or Northern Lights.

Yellowknife

On the north shore of Great Slave Lake, the territorial capital is a modern industrial diamond-mining centre that makes a convenient starting point for exploring the interior. On 21 June there is a Midnight Golf Tournament.

Tuktoyaktuk children

To find out about the customs of the Inuit of the Arctic and the Dene Indians of the Mackenzie Valley, visit the **Prince of Wales Northern Heritage Centre** (daily June–Aug 10.30am–5pm, Sept–May Mon–Fri 10.30am–5pm, Sat–Sun noon–5pm, the archives are Mon–Fri 9am–noon, 1–4.30pm).

For excellent views across the whole town and the lake, head over to the **Bush Pilot's Monument**. Bush pilots will be indispensable if you want to go trout-fishing on Great Bear Lake – which is among the best in the country – or on other remote lakes.

Wood Buffalo National Park

In the southern region of North West Territories there are two spectacular national parks. **Wood Buffalo National Park** is located on either side of the Alberta–Northwest Territories border and was established in 1922 to preserve the bison. This objective has been a success and today the park is home to one of the world's largest free-roaming herds of wood bison. Occupying an area the size of Switzerland – at 44,807 sq km (17,300 sq miles), this is one of the world's largest national parks.

Nahanni National Park

The second national park, further to the west, is located on the Yukon border. **Nahanni National Park**, which is a Unesco World Heritage Site, is in the Deh Cho Region, also known as the Nahanni-Ram, in the vast and remote southwest corner of the NWT. The region was once home to a mysterious band of natives called Nahaa or Nahannis. Legends of wild mountain men, a white queen, evil spirits, lost maps, lost gold and headless men are myths that prevail to this day.

27

Bird enthusiasts are one group that hasn't been deterred from venturing into the Deh Cho. Approximately 280 species of birds have been recorded here, including the threatened trumpeter swan. Visitors can also see impressive river gorges, underground caves and bubbling hot springs. Those who enjoy water travel can journey down the meandering South Nahanni River, one of the wildest rivers in Canada, until they arrive at Virginia Falls, which plunge 90m (295ft), almost twice that of Niagara Falls. Access to the park by road or air is from Fort Simpson.

Nunavut

The Eastern Arctic, including much of the archipelago and the terrain east of Great Slave Lake, remained a hidden world until the age of the

Untamed Nunavut

The delights of Nunavut's great outdoors draw those who can afford the time and money to visit. As there are virtually no roads, other than a 21km (13-mile) stretch between Arctic Bay and Nanisivik, the only travel options are by aircraft, snowmobile or dog-sled. The challenging weather conditions mean frequent delays and changed itineraries. That said, the rewards are infinite.

aeroplane. It became the new territory of Nunavut – which means 'our land' in Inuktitut – on 1 April 1999, when the Northwest Territories were split into two.

Approximately 85 percent of Nunavut's population is Inuit and it had been vying for independence since 1973, fuelled by the desire for a self-governed territory with control over its own future. Canada's newest territory is also its largest, occupying about 20 percent of the country's landmass, almost entirely above the timberline and spread across three time zones. Nunavut extends from the eastern shores of Baffin and Ellesmere islands, west to the plateaux and cliffs of the Arctic Coast on the Coronation Gulf, and north to the High Arctic Islands and the North Pole. It is home to various outpost settlements and 27 communities, the largest of which is the capital, Iqaluit, with a population of around 6,000 citizens.

Irrefutably, Nunavut's main draw is the outdoors, and outfitters arrange packages, from building igloos to polar-bear watching, dog-sledding and encounters with narwhals (one-tusked whales at one time believed to be cousins of the mythical unicorn). Most tourists come during the two-to-three-month sum-

The Polar Bear's Cycle

In summer, polar bears can be seen sailing into Churchill harbour on ice floes. The cruise makes a change from the rigours of seal-hunting on the frozen bay. Once they reach the southern shores of the Hudson Bay, the bears take it easy and switch to a vegetarian diet for a while.

Mating takes place on the pack ice in April and May. After the autumn cruise, the mother moves inland and digs a shelter in the shape of an igloo out of a snowbank. In late December–early January, she gives birth to a cub the size of a guinea pig. In early spring, after hibernation, the bears emerge to hunt for baby seals out on the ice. After two years, when the bear cub is big enough to look after itself, its parents return to Churchill for their holiday.

mer, with its 24 hours of sunshine, when temperatures average 12°C (54°F). Nonetheless, some seasoned adventurers brave the lows of the Arctic winter, when the mercury plummets to –46°C (–51°F), to accompany a traditional Inuit seal hunt or view the spectacular Northern Lights under winter's dark skies.

Hunting for food

Baffin Island

Baffin Island is home to roughly a quarter of Canada's Inuit population and some of the oldest northern communities in the world. **Cape Dorset**, on the southwest coast, is the home of modern Inuit art, the understated simplicity of which expresses the harmonic Inuit vision of Arctic life. Inuit art has been attracting international attention since it was first developed commercially in the 1950s. For action-lovers, Cape Dorset also offers hiking and cross-country skiing tours. **Iqaluit**, on the southeast coast, is the capital of Nunavut and another Baffin Island community rich in Inuit heritage. Here, the Inuit have made extensive walking trails that pass by ancient cairns, built as landmarks.

The **glaciers** on Baffin are another source of inspiration. The Penney Ice Cap is 5,700 sq km (2,200 sq miles) of ice and snow. Sections of Baffin Island's east coast, where there are fjords and spectacular cliffs that rise to 2,100m (6,888ft), higher than the walls of the Grand Canyon, also offer a taste of the Ice Age. During the summer, beluga whales come to frolic around its shores.

WHAT TO DO

In Canada there are so many leisure options, you are spoilt for choice, and the problem is to decide what not to do. The country's huge land and water masses and varied climate provide a wealth of opportunities for outdoor pursuits and sports. Canada's cultural diversity allows for a year-round celebration of the arts and folk traditions from the Old and New World. And, naturally, in a prosperous consumer society, there are innumerable shops.

SPORTS

The country itself is, in a sense, one big outdoor sports facility and the following is just the tip of the iceberg.

Camping

The most popular outdoor Canadian pursuit, camping combines well with other outdoor pursuits. Privately run camp sites offer the most modern conveniences, such as hot showers and electrical appliances, and are particularly appropriate for caravans and camping cars. The national and provincial parks have more modest facilities but are located in attractive sites near lakes and rivers, ideal for camping off the beaten track. You'll find detailed lists of camping facilities on www.travelingcanada.com. For a complete online tour of all the national parks and their possibilities for camping and other sporting activities, visit www.parkscanada.gc.ca.

Hiking

Hiking takes you to the true heart of the country, but remember, leaving civilisation behind is only a pleasure if you are wearing appropriate footwear. In the Rockies, flimsy tennis shoes or trainers

Making the most of nature in Saskatchewan

Whitewater rafting in Québec

won't do. However good the weather is when you set out, pack something waterproof, a sweater for high altitudes or late afternoon, and a spare pair of socks in a small backpack. Before you set off, be sure to get detailed trail maps from park reception centres; and remember that mobile phones often do not work in remote locations.

Mountain Climbing

If you want to go mountain climbing, the best opportunities are in the Coastal Range, in British Columbia, or in the Rockies. While beginners will no doubt prefer the easier slopes of the Laurentians, veterans should head for the higher peaks in the Kluane National Park, in the Yukon.

Canoeing and Rafting

Try **canoeing** on the rivers and lakes (a good way of transporting your equipment to more remote campgrounds, just as the fur traders of old once did). The Iroquois birchbark canoes or Kwakiutl cedar dugout canoes have been replaced by those of modern materials, such as fibreglass, aluminium or hardened rubber, but solid wooden canoes can still be hired in the parks. Beginners start out on a quiet pond; even experienced canoeists stick close to the bank when venturing onto a river. For any prolonged expedition, it is best to go in a group with two or three canoes in case one capsizes.

If you want to go **whitewater rafting**, join a group on the Thompson River in British Columbia (Thompson Okanagan Tourism, tel: 800-567 2275; www.totabc.com). For the Ottawa

River in Ontario, contact a specialist rafting company such as the RiverRun Rafting and Wilderness Resort (tel: 800-267 8504; www.riverrunners.com). If you want to tackle the Lachine Rapids on the St Lawrence in Québec, Lachine Rapids Tours offers a variety of water activities including rafting (tel: 514-284 9607; www.jetboatingmontreal.com).

Fishing

The abundance and variety of Canada's fishing, both deep-sea and freshwater, make it a paradise for anglers. Off the Maritimes, Atlantic tuna, mackerel, cod and swordfish abound, as do the matchless Pacific salmon *(see page 178)* and sea bass along the coast of British Columbia.

In the myriad lakes and rivers that spangle the country from one coast to the other, there are trout of every imaginable species, plus grayling, whitefish, pike and perch. Each province has its own licensing laws, so check on permits and restrictions with local tourist offices and park reception centres.

Bugs and Bears

Luckily, the joys of camping compensate for its drawbacks. The size of Canadian mosquitoes become extremely larger the farther north you go. Black flies are at their worst in June. Things get better in late summer, but whenever possible pitch your tent in an airy, open space. In any case, be sure to arm yourself with plenty of insect repellent.

Bears are another hazard. Don't feed them, and never leave food scraps around the camp. Keep a respectful distance, whether they are black, brown or grizzly bears, adults or cubs. Take your close-up photographs with a telephoto lens, and never use a flash. When in bear territory, don't move about silently; make enough noise for them to know that you're there: they don't like surprises. For more advice on keeping people and bears safe, visit the Canada Trails website, www.canadatrails.co/outdoors/bears.html.

For information on fishing permits and guides visit www.outdoorcanada.ca or www.gofishinontario.com.

Birdwatching

Most parks are a paradise for **birdwatching**, in particular the reserve at Point Pelée (Ontario) and the national parks of Forillon (Gaspé, Québec) and Yoho in the Rockies.

Horse Riding

This is a very popular activity in the west and on the prairies, where novices can improve their technique on a ranch holiday. In Ontario, you'll see more riding caps and white breeches than Stetsons and blue jeans.

Skiing on the slopes

Golf and Tennis

Golf and tennis are best enjoyed away from the big towns, in country resorts such as Montebello and La Malbaie, in Québec; around Georgian Bay and the Muskoka Lakes in Ontario; or outside Victoria on Vancouver Island. In general you will be admitted to a private golf club if you present your home golf club membership card. The website, www.golf-courses.ca provides a list of public and private golf courses in each province.

Watersports

Even a long way from the sea, facilities for watersports are first-rate. **Sailing** and **wind-**

surfing enthusiasts will find near-ideal conditions on Ontario's Georgian Bay, around the Thousand Islands or, more sedately, on the Rideau Canal and the smaller lakes of the Laurentians and Eastern Townships, in Quebec. Sailing is a real obsession from Vancouver to Horseshoe Bay in British Columbia, as well as on the coasts of Nova Scotia. **Swimming** is bracing in the park lakes and rivers, but more relaxed in the warmer waters of the Pacific, especial-ly on the west coast of Van-

Sailing on the lakes

couver Island – where there is the bonus of great waves for **surfing**. On the other side of the country, only the waters of Prince Edward Island's north coast are temperate. One great at-traction on the Nova Scotia coast, south of Halifax, is **diving** for buried treasure, among an estimated 2,000 wrecks.

Winter Sports

To cope with months of cold and snow, Canadians have a wealth of outdoor activities to choose from. Among them, **ice-skating** is a national favourite, with rinks in almost every town, but it's even more fun out in the country, on the frozen lakes, rivers and canals. A popular rink sport, imported from Scotland, is **curl-ing**. Try Inuit-style **ice fishing**, through a hole in the frozen lake. Around Emerald Lake, Banff, Lake Louise and Jasper in the Rockies, the **skiing** – both cross-country and downhill – and snowboarding is world-class. Québec's Laurentian resorts spe-cialise in torch-lit night-skiing. Non-skiers can choose between **snowshoe hiking**, **tobogganing** and **dog-sledding**. Throughout

Eastern Canada there are many fans of the **snowmobile**, for which club membership (day passes are available for tourists) and a driving licence are compulsory.

Spectator Sports

The undisputed king of spectator sports is **ice hockey**: indeed, it's a national obsession from early autumn to late spring. During the 1860s British soldiers garrisoned in Halifax, Nova Scotia, played a primitive form of this fast, brilliantly brutal game; a student of Montréal's McGill University created the game as we know it today in 1879. The Montréal Canadiens team dominated the game for years, but in recent times the power has swung from east to west and back again. In late May and early June, you'll find restaurants and nightclubs strangely empty as people stay at home to watch the televised play-offs and finals of the game's supreme trophy, the Stanley Cup (donated in 1893 by the Governor General, Lord Stanley). The National Hockey League includes American teams, but that doesn't bother people – as their best players are Canadians. By contrast, **Canadian football**, almost indistinguishable from the American game, is dominated by American players.

In summer, American **baseball** is big in Toronto and Montréal, while in Victoria and Vancouver **cricket** prevails. **Rodeo** is a great summer attraction, not only at the Calgary Stampede, but all across Manitoba, Saskatchewan, Alberta and British Columbia. From a word meaning 'roundup', the rodeo demonstrates the skills needed to gather livestock for counting and branding. Bronco-busting, bull-riding, milking wild cows: the tests follow each other in quick succession. In one of them, a cowboy leaps from his galloping horse to bring down a running steer by seizing its horns and twisting it to the ground: the winner is the fastest.

Soccer fans

Soccer (or football as the rest of the world calls it) is becoming hugely popular in Canada. It hosted the FIFA U-20 World Cup in 2007 and will host the 2015 Women's World Cup.

Bespoke hats in a Toronto boutique

SHOPPING

The sense of commerce that founded this nation is still strong, although the fortified trading posts on Hudson Bay, the Great Lakes and St Lawrence River have been replaced by giant shopping malls and a labyrinth of subterranean galleries. Just as the wily Scots of the Hudson's Bay Company tempted the First Nations to settle around the trading posts, so merchants of renovated historic neighbourhoods, entice shoppers into a maze of multi-level stores apparently designed to give them little hope of emerging empty-handed.

Canada's modern **shopping malls** are microcosms of the world market, and nowhere is this more true than at the monumental West Edmonton Shopping Mall *(see page 194)*. In the big cities, most major French, Italian, American and Japanese designers of women's and men's fashions either have their own boutiques or special counters in the department stores. Designer clothes prices are comparable to those in the US. At **outlet shopping malls**, name brands sell clothing, shoes, china and more, at dramatically reduced prices. Check the local newspapers for details of special deals. Europeans should check when buying **electronic goods** that they are compatible with the voltage at home.

The two major **department stores**, Sears and The Bay (Hudson's), are comparable in quality and price. If you're looking for furs and leather goods, The Bay's centuries-old tradition gives it an edge. The company's blanket, which once won the hearts of the Natives, is still regarded as a prestige item.

All the major cities have some kind of **flea market**, usually at weekends in the renovated areas around the docklands. But many of the most enjoyable ones are out in the depths of the country, from BC's interior to Québec's Eastern Townships.

In this land of the great outdoors, hunting jackets and parkas are ruggedly efficient and offer excellent protection against the elements without attempting to be fashionable: they are particularly good in Québec and New Brunswick. In Alberta and British Columbia, look for cowboy clothes – hand-tooled boots, belts and Stetson hats. In Newfoundland, you might want to invest in fishermen's oilskins and sou'wester hats in yellow or black.

More and more shops are specialising in high-quality native crafts. The best clothes buys are Inuit *mukluks* (fur-and-sealskin boots), moccasins, mittens, and heavy-knit Cowichan sweaters (on the west coast). The First Nations make fine basketry, beadwork and silver jewellery, excelling at black argillite and wood carvings; the Inuit specialise in soapstone, onyx, bone and scrimshaw (etched ivory) sculpture. In Montréal, you'll find good examples of this work at the Canadian Guild of Crafts (1460 rue Sherbrooke Ouest). As a general rule, your best chance of finding high-quality craftwork is in the museum shops, notably at Vancouver's Museum of Anthropology, Toronto's Royal Ontario Museum, the McMichael Canadian Art Collection, near Toronto, and the Glenbow Museum in Calgary. Don't forget the craftwork of Canada's European cultures (quilts, rag dolls, rugs, needlework, ceramics), still to be found in country towns.

ENTERTAINMENT

After years of fighting an uphill battle against the competitive lures of the United States and Europe, Canada's performing arts have come into their own.

Theatre in particular has staked out a place for itself on the North American scene with, among others, Ontario's prestigious Stratford Shakespeare Festival and the George Bernard Shaw Festival in Niagara-on-the-Lake. Your travel agent or the Canada tourism office can help you book in advance for these highly popular summer events, which include light comedies and musicals along with the more serious fare. Toronto encourages contemporary Canadian drama at the St Lawrence Centre for the Performing Arts and at many smaller theatres, and stages large-scale musicals at the Royal Alexandra Theatre, the Princess of Wales Theatre and the Canon Theatre.

In Montréal and Québec City, theatre aficionados enjoy

Curtain up at the Vancouver Playhouse

Ballet in Montréal

French-Canadian dramas presented with flare and sophistication. French-speakers in Québec appreciate the caustic wit of its **cabaret** artists and the nostalgic **folk songs** in the *boîtes à chansons* (folk song clubs) along the city's Grande Allée and around rue St-Denis in Montréal.

When it comes to **classical music**, Canada has two orchestras of international repute: the Montréal Symphony performs at Place des Arts and the Toronto Symphony at Roy Thomson Hall. Meanwhile, the Vancouver, Winnipeg and Edmonton orchestras are growing in stature. If you are in Vieux-Montréal in summer, look for the organ recitals in Notre-Dame.

Canada has always figured prominently in the world of **dance**. Among the most renowned companies are Toronto's National Ballet of Canada, Les Grands Ballets Canadiens of Montréal, the Royal Winnipeg Ballet and Alberta Ballet in Calgary. Performances by these companies – like **opera** performances in Toronto, Ottawa and Montréal – are mainly confined to winter. In summer there are occasional shows in the city parks.

Jazz can be heard in pubs and clubs, in cities and beyond, and also during the international festivals such as those of Montréal and Vancouver. The vibrant Toronto jazz scene includes two annual festivals and many outstanding jazz venues, among them a variety of jazz cruises around the Toronto Islands. For more information visit the website www.toronto.com. In summer the country's major sports stadia resonate to the sound of **rock concerts**. Scottish **bagpipe music** and **highland dancing** are specialities in Nova Scotia. You'll find both in abundance in Halifax and on Cape Breton Island.

Festivals and Events

Parades and street parties across the country commemorate Canada's brief but varied history. Ethnic communities put on traditional costumes for annual pageants. Here is a selection of folklore and cultural festivities:

January *Vancouver* New Year's Day Polar Bear Swim in the ocean. *Montréal* Igloofest – the ultimate outdoor winter rave.

February *Montréal* Highlights Festival. *Québec City* Winter Carnival – ice-sculpture competition, canoe races, costumed pageant, torchlight skiing. *Vancouver* Chinese New Year.

March/April *Eastern Townships (Québec)* 'Sugaring off' parties. *Niagara-on-the-Lake* Shaw Festival: plays by George Bernard Shaw.

May *Toronto* Hot Docs International Film Festival. *Ottawa* Festival of Spring – tulips, fireworks and beer gardens. *Nationwide (except Québec)* Queen Victoria's birthday (24 May) – fireworks. *Ottawa* Canadian Tulip Festival. *Vancouver* International Children's Festival. *Banff* Summer Arts Festival (until September)

June *Stratford (Ontario)* Shakespeare Festival and *Charlottetown (Prince Edward Island)* Summer Festival (both until October). *Montréal* International Jazz Festival. *Yellowknife* Midnight Sun Golf Classic (21 June). *Québec* Fête Nationale – bonfires, parades, street dances (24 June). *Halifax (Nova Scotia)* Tattoo, a Scottish pageant.

July *Nationwide* Canada Day (1 July), *Ottawa* fireworks and variety show. *Montréal* Just-For-Laughs Festival (Festival du Rire) – international clowns and comedians in English and French. *Calgary* Stampede. *Edmonton* Klondike Days. *Saint John (New Brunswick)* Loyalist Days – 18th-century costumed pageant.

August *Montréal* World Film Festival. *Clare* Festival acadien de clare, Nova Scotia. *Dawson City (Yukon)* Discovery Day (17 August). *St John's (Newfoundland)* Regatta on Quidi Vidi Lake. *Winnipeg* Folklorama. *Regina* Queen City Ex – horse-racing, barbecues, brass bands and street dances.

September *St Catharines (Ontario)* Niagara Wine Festival for Niagara Peninsula wineries.

October *Kitchener (Ontario)* Oktoberfest. *Vancouver* International Film Festival.

December *Niagara Falls* Winter Festival of Lights around the Falls.

EATING OUT

Canada's culinary heritage spans almost 5,000 miles (8,000km) and many centuries, beginning with its First Nations. From the 17th century onwards, immigrants from Great Britain, France and the rest of Europe brought with them recipes that were adapted to suit the foods they discovered in their new homeland. In more recent years, the combination of greater affluence, more travel abroad, the influx of more immigrants from every corner of the world, and regional pride in fresh local products has created a generation with more discerning palates than ever before.

The range of cuisine is varied and interesting, from Pacific salmon to Atlantic lobster, Alberta beef to Yukon moose, Ontario pheasant to Québec bison. In urban areas, there are plentiful international choices as well as what is considered to be more traditional fare. From Italian to Russian, Chinese to Brazilian, Canada offers a veritable smorgasbord of tastes and flavours.

To be sure, you'll come across some of the bland Anglo-Saxon cooking of days gone by, frequently in the average middle-of-the-road restaurant, just as you will south of the border. From one end of the Trans-Canada Highway to the other, you may find the same straightforward vegetable soups with a suspiciously familiar canned flavour, plain green salads, steak and potatoes, fruit pies and ice cream. But there are now many more inventive, spicier alternatives. Québec's authentic French Canadian cuisine ranges from such traditional fare as richly spiced *tortière* and maple sugar pie to modern delicacies based on specific regional ingredients – from duck *fois gras* to fine local cheeses. On the other side of the country, many of British Columbia's

Casual dining

People don't feel obliged to dress up to eat out in Canada. Only in the smartest restaurants do men sometimes have to wear a tie.

restaurants are trendsetters, creating concoctions ranging from edible flowers to fusion – an ever-changing blend of Asian flavours with British Columbian ingredients.

Breakfast

As soon as you sit down to breakfast (served between 7am and 11am), you'll see the waitress approaching you with a pot of coffee. Serving coffee is the way of saying 'welcome', and you will need to be very firm to prevent this automatic gesture if you don't want coffee immediately or if you prefer tea. By European standards, hotel coffee is often weak, but your cup will be refilled several times.

Welcoming cups of coffee

As a general rule, you have the choice of a continental breakfast of toast and assorted pastries, croissants or muffins, plus fruit juice and coffee or tea; or an American-British style breakfast, which includes, in addition, cereal, eggs, waffles or pancakes with maple syrup, and sausages or lean Canadian back bacon. This last regional treat is best of all as the lower layer of an 'eggs Benedict' on an English muffin with poached egg and sauce hollandaise. In some diners (small simple restaurants), they may also serve fish and steak for the morning meal.

Lunch

On an active sightseeing day, adopt the Canadian habit of a simple sandwich for lunch. A favourite is the French version of the submarine or hero, a big, mouth-stretching sandwich of French bread filled with meatballs, sausages or ham, cheese, salami, onions, sweet peppers, lettuce and tomatoes. You won't want a dessert after one of these. Salads and hearty soups are a popular alternative to a sandwich.

Dinner

The evening meal begins on the early side, around 6.30 or 7pm, although service continues until about 10.30pm. Disconcertingly for people used to European cuisine, salad may be served before the main dish. Salad dressings can be surprising concoctions and not to everyone's taste. If you would prefer a simple vinaigrette dressing, you can always ask the waiter to bring you oil, vinegar and a little mustard, and mix your own.

Canadian dress habits are generally fairly relaxed, and it's only the most dauntingly smart restaurants that expect men to wear a tie and women a dress or dressy trousers rather than jeans.

REGIONAL SPECIALITIES

The growing interest in reducing their environmental footprint has reminded Canadians of the great natural riches they possess, not only in their national and provincial parks but also at their dinner tables. If you're travelling across the country, don't settle for the standard fare; seek out some of the local delicacies.

Atlantic Canada. Nova Scotia, Prince Edward Island and New Brunswick are all justly proud of their lobster, best served at its simplest – boiled, steamed, or grilled with a little lemon butter on the side – on the proper assumption that the meat is too good to be submerged in any fancy tomato or cream sauce. In this grand culinary rivalry, PEI offers its Malpeque oysters, fresh, stewed or in a bisque soup; Nova Scotia counters with fried Digby scallops and clam chowder, a spicy soup made with onions, potatoes and milk. New Brunswick proposes broiled salmon and shad *amandine* (with sliced almonds). Meanwhile, Newfoundland performs neat little miracles with its cod, using everything from the roe to the cheeks and tongue. PEI's potato pancakes lend new dignity to a basic dish.

More exotic regional delicacies include New Brunswick's fiddlehead, an edible fern served steamed with roast lamb, and dulse, a chewy dried seaweed; and Nova Scotia's solomon gundy (a derivation of salmagundi), a mixture of chopped meat and pickled herring in oil, vinegar, pepper and onions. PEI produces its own version of Gouda cheese, and delicious hand-made chocolates. For dessert, try the blueberry and rhubarb pies and fresh strawberries of Nova Scotia and New Brunswick. In Newfoundland, choose the unique, amber-coloured bakeapple berry, rich in vitamin C.

Québec. The province's heart-warming pea soup *(soupe aux pois)*, made with yellow peas, is best when enriched with a ham hock. A good onion soup *(soupe à l'oignon)* may be harder to find. Québécois cooking, which has its origins in that of Norman and Breton peasants, is rustic and unpretentious. Pork and maple sugar are

Fish is at its best in the Atlantic provinces

British Columbia's Okanagan Valley is renowned for its fruit

basic elements. Among the most common dishes are *cretons* (pork pâté), *andouillette aux fines herbes* (pork-tripe sausage), and *fèves au lard* (bacon-flavoured pork and beans). Maple syrup is used in curing ham, on scrambled eggs, and in sauces for wild game, notably the fine partridge, grouse and Canada goose. *Tourtière* is a pie filled with venison, partridge or hare and finely chopped potatoes. *Cipaille* is a dish of game and potatoes arranged into six layers divided by puff pastry. Typical snacks include *poutine,* French fries covered with melted cheese and gravy, and *guedille,* salad in a hot-dog bun. Two of the country's best cheeses are the blue Ermite and Italian-style ricotta made by the Benedictine monks of St-Benoît-du-Lac in the Eastern Townships.

Another speciality, which is typical of Montréal, is the smoked meat sandwich served on rye bread with pickled cucumbers and coleslaw. They try to match it in Toronto and Vancouver, but members of the English-speaking diaspora that left Montréal in the 1970s still return on pilgrimages for the smoked meat on boulevard St-Laurent.

Ontario. The province's countless lakes make freshwater fish – trout, whitefish, and pike – the pride of the Ontario table. The fish are often baked in wines of the Niagara Peninsula. In this great hunting country, roast pheasant in maple syrup is a noted delicacy. Around Niagara-on-the-Lake, the Loyalist tradition is upheld with a pumpkin pie considered superior to anything produced south of the border. The quality and range of Toronto's restaurants is astonishingly good, due to the arrival of immigrants from countries such as Italy, Greece, China and, more recently, India, Korea and Thailand.

The Prairies. Wildfowl and corn-fed farm poultry are delicious in Manitoba and Saskatchewan. Try roast turkey served with red cabbage and a sauce of locally grown cranberries. Baked partridge and roast wild duck are superb. The corn on the cob makes a great lunch on its own.

Freshwater fish include baked lake trout and broiled pickerel, while Manitoba's caviar served with sour cream would impress many a purist. Smoked goldeye and baked, stuffed whitefish come from Lake Winnipeg.

Alberta's beef is justly celebrated: superb when grilled, it is also delicious in a traditional stew. Calgary's steak houses are excellent, but Europeans may be disconcerted to see steak and lobster occasionally served together, a combination known as 'surf and turf'. Barbecued chicken and ribs are a more universally accepted combination. Buffalo steaks are uncommonly juicy, and rack of lamb and leg of pork are other ranch favourites.

Among desserts made from the numerous wild berries, be sure to try the slightly tart Saskatoon berry pie. A great breakfast favourite is hot biscuits with Dauphin honey.

British Columbia. Pacific salmon is the pride and joy of the province as a whole and Vancouver in particular. Always simply prepared, it is equally

Sweet treats

Don't miss the uniquely Canadian and ubiquitous butter tarts: pastry shells filled with a sticky mixture of butter, sugar, maple syrup and sometimes raisins or pecan nuts.

superb baked or grilled. The shrimp, crab, black cod and halibut are among the best in North America.

The freshness and variety of the seafood make the province's Japanese restaurants a special attraction for some of the best *sashimi* and *sushi* outside Japan. By the same token, in Vancouver's wonderful Chinese restaurants the seafood dishes are undoubtedly the star turns.

The lamb reared on Saltspring Island is exquisite roasted with mint sauce, and British Columbia's chefs prepare it in many innovative ways, complementing it with other fresh local produce.

Even though the gastronomic revival has not yet reached the North, gourmets and hunters – the two often go together – insist that the best moose steaks in Canada come from the forests of the Yukon (it is cooked medium-rare and served with a baked

Sweet Maple

Maple sugar and syrup are uniquely North American products, with forests of the Maple Belt stretching from the American Midwest across to the Canadian Maritimes. Québec accounts for more than 90 percent of Canadian production. In the autumn, the maple concentrates its sugars in the 'rays' of tubular cells under the bark. After maturing through the winter, the sugar sap begins to flow with the first warm days of spring. Traditionally, holes are bored into the trunk to tap the flow through a pipe into a waiting bucket. Alternating freezing night temperatures and warmer days cause a pumping action that continues to produce buckets of sap for up to six weeks. The sap is boiled down in wood-fired vats and evaporated into syrup. About 150 litres (39 Imperial gallons) of sap produce nearly 4 litres (just under 1 gallon) of maple syrup.

Although modern industrial methods have replaced most of the old buckets with a more hygienic vacuum-tubing system to tap the sap directly into the vats, the buckets are still used as part of the ritual of the 'sugaring-off' parties that are held to celebrate the end of the long, hard, Québec winter and the coming of spring.

potato). If you are not able to get to the Yukon, moose is sometimes served in the British Columbian interior and in both northern Ontario and Québec. You should try to sample it at least once in your lifetime.

The best of British Columbia's desserts are quite simply the fresh fruits of the Okanagan Valley's – peaches, apricots and apples (the latter are extemely good eaten in the English style, accompanied by the local Armstrong cheddar cheese).

Blessed Church wine, made in Vancouver

DRINKS

Canada's national drink is beer: 'It's all those lakes and rivers that make it so great.' Served ice-cold, it is closer in strength and flavour to German or Belgian beer than the milder American version. By contrast, the cider is considerably less potent than the European brew.

Canada's two main wine regions, on Ontario's Niagara Penninsula and in BC's Okanagan Valley, are producing many wines that are earning international acclaim. The vines must be tough to resist the glacial winters and occasional late May frosts. French, Italian, German and American wines are available in big city restaurants, but prices are high – except in tax-free Alberta, where you can afford a decent Bordeaux with your steak.

In Québec, they'll pay the price. They'll also mix red wine with hard liquor and call it a caribou, a truly gut-warming cocktail for the long winter nights. The connoisseur's drink here is Canadian rye whisky, best sipped, they say, neat and without ice.

A–Z TRAVEL TIPS

A Summary of Practical Information

A

ACCOMMODATION

Many of the provincial tourist authorities inspect and grade accommodation annually. Official directories of establishments, available free of charge, give full details of facilities and services. Booking three or four months ahead during the high season (December to March for ski resorts, June to September for summer travel) is always advisable. Alberta, tel: 800-252 3782, http://travelalberta.com; British Columbia, tel: 800-435 5622, www.hellobc.com; Manitoba, tel: 800-665 0040, www.travelmanitoba.com; New Brunswick, tel: 800-561 0123, www.tourismnewbrunswick.ca; Newfoundland and Labrador, tel: 800-563 6353, www.newfoundlandlabrador.com; Northwest Territories, tel: 800-661 0788, www.spectacularnwt.com; Nova Scotia, tel: 800-565 0000, www.novascotia.com; Nunavut, tel: 866-686 2888, www.nunavuttourism.com; Ontario, tel: 800-668 2746, www.ontariotravel.net; Prince Edward Island, tel: 800-463 4734, outside of North America, tel: 902-368 4444, www.gov.pe.ca/visitorsguide; Québec, tel: 877-266 5687, www.bonjourquebec.com; Saskatchewan, tel: 877-237 2273, www.sasktourism.com; Yukon, tel: 800-661 0494, www.travelyukon.com.

Hotels. Many chains and individual hotels offer reduced rates at weekends and during off-peak season for families and senior citizens. You can make nationwide reservations through the free booking services operated by most chains.

Resort hotels offer special rates to guests who take their meals on the premises. AP (American Plan) includes three meals a day and MAP (Modified American Plan) includes breakfast and lunch or dinner. On the European Plan (EP), no meals are provided.

Motels. Often situated near highways and main access roads, motels are a popular choice for tourists travelling by car.

Bed and breakfast. Great for families and budget travellers, bed-

and-breakfast accommodation – often a room or two with shared or private bath in a family home – allows you to meet Canadians while you save money. Provincial and territorial tourist offices have the addresses of local bed-and-breakfast associations, and some will make reservations for you.

Camps and lodges. Camps and lodges are often located in remote areas and specialise in hunting, fishing or naturalist activities such as watching wildlife and birds. Accommodation may be in cabins or cottages. Some establishments have private bath and/or cooking facilities, while others have a separate building with dining room and washing facilities.

Country holidays. Stay on a working farm or ranch and take part in seasonal activities – haymaking, lambing and the like – or simply relax in a peaceful rural setting. Some farms and ranches organise hunting and fishing trips, horse riding, hayrides, cross-country skiing, sleigh rides and other activities. Lodgings may be with the farm or ranch family, or in separate accommodation on the grounds. Where meals are not provided, they are usually available on request. Don't miss the chance to sample farm-fresh produce, home-raised beef, lamb and poultry, and home-baked bread, pancakes and berry pie. The provincial tourist offices *(see page 248)* will also be able to provide in-depth information on country holidays.

AIRPORTS

The following are some of the major, full-service airports in Canada. For a full listing of Canadian airports visit www.cacairports.ca.

Calgary. *Calgary International YYC*, 18km (11 miles) outside the city centre. Airport buses, shuttles and other public transport circulate frequently between town and airport, stopping at the major hotels. Taxis are always on hand for the trip into Calgary. Several coach services operate from the airport to Banff and Lake Louise. Tel: 403-735 1200, www.calgaryairport.com.

Halifax. *Halifax Stanfield International YHZ*, 42km (26 miles) from the city. Numerous ground transport services, such as the 'Airporter', which provides a shuttle service to and from various hotels in the metro area, are available at the kerbside in the domestic arrival area. For general information, tel: 902-873 4422, www.hiaa.ca.

Montréal. Operated by Aéroports de Montréal, *Pierre Elliott Trudeau International Airport YUL*, 20km (12 miles) from the city centre, handles both North American and international flights. Airport buses travel to major downtown hotels, and to the centre. Taxis are also available, as are local buses that connect with the subway. Aéroports de Montréal customer service: tel: 514-394 7377, or 800-4651213, www.admtl.com.

Edmonton. *Edmonton International YEG*, 29km (18 miles) from the city centre. Many hotels in the city offer complimentary shuttle service to and from the airport. There is also shuttle service to and from other parts of the city, including the West Edmonton Mall. For more information on shuttle services, call 780-465 8515. No city buses serve the airport. Airport tel: 780-890 8900, www.flyeia.

Ottawa. *Ottawa International YOW*, 10km (6 miles) south of the city centre. A variety of transport options are available to and from the airport, including limousine, taxi and hotel shuttle service. For public transport, call 613-741 4390, www.octranspo.com. Airport tel: 613-248 2000, www.ottawa-airport.ca.

Toronto. *Toronto Pearson International*, 30km (18 miles) from the city centre. Transport to and from the airport is available to many destination points both near and far. In addition to the GO Transit bus, travellers have several other public transport options to and from the city centre, including Mississauga Transit, Airport Express and TTC. Pacific Western buses, which operate Airport Express, run between the airport and Islington, Yorkdale and York Mills underground (subway) stations. Alternatively, you can take a limousine or taxi into town. Airport tel: 416-776 3843, www.gtaa.com.

Toronto Islands. *Billy Bishop Toronto City Airport YTZ* is linked by a two-minute ferry service (every 15 minutes) to the foot of

Bathurst Street and the downtown core, including taxi services and TTC. Two airlines, Porter and Air Canada, fly to over 15 Canadian and US cities US from this airport. Airport tel: 416-203 6942, www.torontoport. com/airport.asp.

Vancouver. *Vancouver International YVR*, 18km (11 miles) from the city centre. Transport to and from the airport is available in many forms. Since 2010 Canada Line has offered a rapid transit link from the airport to downtown Vancouver and Richmond. Bus services include Airporter, Airport Link, Pacific Coach Lines, Perimeter's Whistler Express and Quick Shuttle, all serving different points in and around the city. There are also courtesy shuttles, limousines and plenty of taxis. Airport tel: 604-207 7077, www.yvr.ca.

B

BICYCLE RENTAL

Bicycle rentals are available in most large Canadian cities. Vancouver, Toronto, Ottawa and Montréal each have cycle paths that are as popular with visitors as with locals. BIXI bicycle rentals are in Montréal (tel: 514-789 2949 or 877-820 2453, https://montreal.bixi.com; in Ottawa (https://capital.bixi.com) and in Toronto (tel: 877-412 2494, https://toronto.bixi.com). In Vancouver, there are numerous bicycle rental companies located close to Stanley Park, along Denman and Davie streets, including English Bay Bike Rentals, tel: 604-568 8490 and Stanley Park Cycle, tel: 604-688 0087.

BUDGETING FOR YOUR TRIP

Accommodation and food. The daily costs for an average traveller in Canada varies considerably across the country. In the large cities – Vancouver, Toronto, and Montréal – the comfortable daily cost should be about $250 ($170 for hotel, $10 for breakfast, $20 for lunch, $40 for dinner and $10 for public transport). Accommodation and food costs generally decrease away from the main centres, except in the far North. A thrifty traveller in the city – and an average traveller in more rural areas – might get away with about $160–185 per day ($100–125 for accommodations, $50 for restaurant food, or as little as $20 self-catering and $10 for fares). For extravagant luxury in the city – and in hot spots such as Banff, Whistler, and Mont Tremblant – you could pay $700–800 per day ($300–500 for accommodation, $25 for breakfast, $75 for lunch, as much as $200 for dinner and $100 for taxi fares). Other costs of note: a bottle of wine in a restaurant will generally cost from $16, beer $5–6, cocktails from $6.

Public transport. Underground (subway), bus, tram or trolleybus $2.50 and up. Series of tickets and monthly passes are available at lower rates.

Taxis. Starting tariff $3, plus at least $1 per km on average.

C

CAMPING

Canada has thousands of campsites, including national, provincial, municipal and privately-run sites in parks, cities and towns. A network of sites spans the length of major highways, with many campsites situated both on well-travelled routes and in more remote areas. As well as toilets, showers and hook-ups for RVs (Recreational Vehicles, or campers), laundry, cooking and sports facilities may be provided. Parks Canada website, www.parkscanada.ca, tel: 888-773 8888, provides information for camping in national parks as well as links to the official provincial tourist websites which provide information on camping in the provinces. More information can be obtained by going to www.travelingcanada.com.

Warning: Outside urban areas, insects can be voracious in late spring and summer. Have repellent on hand, as well as netting for tents and screens for RVs. In many areas, temperatures can plummet at night, even in summer. Be sure you have enough bedding and warm clothing. People can and do get lost in remote areas, so inform others of your whereabouts and expected time of return.

CAR HIRE

Cars and campers (RVs) can be hired at major airports (24-hour service) and seaports, and in many towns and cities. Numerous local firms vie with the well-known international companies, keeping prices competitive. It's a good idea to book well in advance for the peak tourist period. Always ask about special offers and package arrangements, including reasonable weekend or monthly rates.

Payment is usually by credit card. Otherwise, the customer is required to make a substantial cash deposit. Some firms may refuse to hire cars if the customer does not have a credit card. Some set the minimum age at 21, others at 25. A surcharge may be levied if you hire a car in one city and leave it in another.

Call the following firms, toll-free, for information: **Avis Canada** tel: 800-230 4898, www.avis.ca; **Budget** tel: 800-268 8900, www.budget.ca; **Discount Car and Truck Rentals** tel: 800-263 2355, www.discountcar.com; **Hertz** tel: 1-800-654 3131, www.hertz.ca; **Thrifty** tel: 800-847 4389, www.thrifty.com.

CLIMATE AND CLOTHING

Canada's climate varies tremendously with the season and the latitude – ranging from the temperate south to the ice-bound Arctic Circle. Summers are short but hot over much of the country, with milder, rainier weather year-round on the Pacific coast. Bring plenty of layering clothes, plus lightweight woollens and a raincoat, if you plan to make a visit to British Columbia. The far north warms up during the summer months, though it cools down at night and remains chilly in the early morning. Dress in layers for maximum comfort.

Winters are severe almost everywhere. Bring a heavy overcoat, snow boots, hat, scarf and gloves, as well as clothes for winter sports.

Monthly average maximum and minimum daytime temperatures in degrees Fahrenheit:

		J	F	M	A	M	J	J	A	S	O	N	D
Toronto	max.	30	31	40	53	64	75	80	78	71	60	46	34
	min.	18	19	27	38	47	57	62	61	54	45	35	23
Edmonton	max.	5	31	40	53	64	75	80	78	71	60	46	34
	min.	-2	7	3	30	41	50	54	52	43	32	18	5
Vancouver	max.	41	44	50	58	64	69	74	73	65	57	48	43
	min.	32	34	37	40	46	52	54	54	49	44	39	35

And in degrees Celsius:

		J	F	M	A	M	J	J	A	S	O	N	D
Toronto	max.	-1	-3	4	12	18	24	27	26	22	15	8	1
	min.	-8	-7	-3	3	8	14	16	16	12	7	2	-4
Edmonton	max.	-15	-10	-9	4	11	15	17	16	11	6	-4	-10
	min.	-19	-14	-16	-1	5	10	12	11	6	0	-8	-15
Vancouver	max.	5	7	10	14	18	21	23	23	18	14	9	6
	min.	0	1	3	4	8	11	12	12	9	7	4	2

CRIME AND SAFETY

Incidents of urban violence and street crime are rare in Canada. People walk about comfortably after dark in the country's town centres. Nevertheless, it's always good to take a few common-sense precautions. Avoid badly lit or run-down areas at night. Store any valuables and reserves of cash in the hotel safe. Be sure to lock your car and hotel room. Keep a photocopy of your plane tickets and other personal documents, with a note of the phone number of your travel agent; they could come in handy in case of loss or theft. If you see a crime being committed and you want to report it, you can call Crime

Stoppers (*Échec au crime*). Crime Stoppers is a national organisation dedicated to serving Canadians by making it possible for those who have information concerning a crime to contact the police and still remain anonymous. Tel: 800-222 TIPS (8477).

D

DISABLED TRAVELLERS

The Canadian Transportation Agency offers an on-line guide for disabled visitors travelling by air in Canada, which can be accessed at www.cta-otc.gc.ca.

Airlines, buses, and trains all offer wheelchair assistance, although you should allow extra time before commencing your journey. Taking a wheelchair on the train requires advanced notice so it in recommended to call VIA Rail 48 hours beforehand (toll free tel: 888-842 7245, www.viarail.ca).

DRIVING

Crossing the border. Cars registered in the United States may be brought into Canada by the owner or his/her authorised driver for the duration of its registration period. The necessary formalities can be taken care of at the border.

US visitors taking a car into Canada will need:

• A valid US driver's licence
• Car registration papers
• Interprovince Motor Vehicle Liability
• Insurance Card or evidence of sufficient insurance coverage to conform with local laws (available from an insurance agent)

An international driving permit is highly recommended for visitors from non-English-speaking countries.

Breakdowns. If you have a breakdown, pull over onto the shoulder, raise the bonnet, and wait for help – or walk to the nearest roadside emergency telephone. The Canadian Automobile Association

(CAA) provides members and international affiliates with some breakdown assistance and travel information (itineraries, maps, guide books), as well as the services of an accommodation reservations desk and travel agency. For further information, contact the Canadian Automobile Association, tel: 800-222-4357, www.caa.ca.

Road signs are either in French or English, or use self-explanatory symbols. If you do find yourself in an exclusively French-speaking area, here are the most common written ones and some useful phrases:

Arrêt	Stop
Attention	Caution
Cédez	Give way
Défense de stationner	No parking
Ecole/Ecoliers	School/Schoolchildren
Lentement	Slow
Piétons	Pedestrians
Réparations	Road work
Sortie de camions	Truck exit
Stationnement	Parking
Sommes-nous sur la route de…?	Are we on the road to…?
Faites le plein, s'il vous plaît.	Fill the tank, please.
Vérifiez l'huile/les pneus/la batterie.	Check the oil/tyres/battery.
Ma voiture est en panne.	My car has broken down.

On the road. Drive on the right, pass on the left; give right of way to vehicles coming from your right at unmarked intersections. Traffic signs display the standard international pictographs. Speed limits are given in kilometres. Maximum speed on most highways and expressways is 100km/h (60 mph), on other roads 80km/h (50 mph), in towns 50km/h (30 mph), and near schools and parks 30km/h (20 mph). The use of seat belts is obligatory throughout Canada. It is illegal to drive while under the influence of alcohol. If you surpass the acceptable limit you risk a stiff fine, imprisonment, or both.

E

ELECTRICITY

The current is 110–120 volts, 60-cycle AC. Plugs are the two-prong American type, so other visitors should buy an adapter before they leave for Canada if they bring in electrical appliances.

EMBASSIES AND CONSULATES

The embassies, high commissions and consulates listed below are all to be found in Ottawa.

Australia: High Commission, Suite 710, 50 O'Connor Street, Ottawa, Ontario, K1P 6L2; tel: 613-236 0841 or 888-990 8888, www.canada.embassy.gov.au/otwa/home.html.

Great Britain: High Commission, 80 Elgin Street, Ottawa, Ontario, K1P 5K7; tel: 613-237 1530, http://ukincanada.fco.gov.uk/en.

Ireland: Embassy of Ireland, Suite 1105, 130 Albert Street, Ottawa, Ontario, K1P 5G4; tel: 613-233 6281.

New Zealand: High Commission, Metropolitan House, Suite 727, 99 Bank Street, Ottawa, Ontario, K1P 6G3; tel: 613-238-5991, www.nzembassy.com.

South Africa: High Commission, 15 Sussex Drive, Ottawa, Ontario, K1M 1M8; tel: 613-744-0330, www.southafrica-canada.ca.

US: Consular Section, US Embassy, 490 Sussex Drive, Ottawa, Ontario K1N 1G8, tel: 613-238 5335, http://canada.usembassy.gov.

EMERGENCIES

In the cities, dial '911' for emergency calls to the police, fire department or ambulance service. Elsewhere, dial '0' for the operator, who will contact the appropriate emergency service. In summer, urgent messages can be sent to travellers in Canada via the

'Tourist Alert' programme operated in conjunction with the Royal Canadian Mounted Police. RCMP National Headquarters, tel: 613-993 7267, www.rcmp-grc.gc.ca.

F

FISHING AND HUNTING REGULATIONS

To fish in Canada's lakes and rivers, non-residents must have a permit, issued by the various provincial governments and valid only within the province of issue. Permits are normally available at sporting goods stores, fishing camps and marinas. Separate licences might be required for certain species of fish. In British Columbia, freshwater fishing licences are administered by the Ministry of Environment, tel: 877-855 3222, email: frontcounterbc@gov.bc.ca. Fisheries and Oceans Canada, tel: 613-993 0999, email: info@dfo-mpo.gc.ca, www.pac.dfo-mpo.gc.ca/recfish/licensing, handles licences for saltwater fishing.

Anglers in national parks require a separate licence, available from Parks Canada offices, tel: 888-773 8888, www.pc.gc.ca, and valid in all national parks where fishing is permitted.

The provinces also control hunting permits, except for the federal migratory game bird licence. Apply for the latter at any post office. Non-residents may be required to hire an official guide for hunting and fishing. Open seasons, bag limits and other restrictions vary according to province, so check with the authorities in the area you plan to visit. The tourist information office will be able to put you in contact with the appropriate agency.

G

GAY AND LESBIAN TRAVELLERS

Canada is one of the world's more gay-friendly countries, and in July 2005 became the fourth country to recognize gay marriage, after the Netherlands, Belgium and Spain. For a comprehensive, all-in-one spot to start research, Travel Gay Canada, www.travelgay canada.com provides Canada-wide information on hotels, events and travel packages.

GETTING THERE

By air. Air service is available from most major European cities to one or more of the following Canadian gateway cities: Halifax, Montréal, Toronto, Winnipeg, Calgary, Edmonton and Vancouver.

Frequent flights connect the major US cities and some European capitals to centres across Canada. Flying time from London to Toronto is 7½ hours, from New York 1½ hours. The journey from London to Vancouver takes 9½ hours (7 hours from New York). The largest Canadian air carrier is Air Canada, tel: 888-247 2262, www.aircanada. com (among many other things, this site has an extensive list of international contact numbers for Air Canada). Travel operators feature many charter flights and package tours, including city stays, camping holidays, adventure tours and northern expeditions. Hotel accommodation and car/RV hire is often included in the package.

By sea. Marine Atlantic ferries carry cars and passengers between Bar Harbor, Maine and Yarmouth, Nova Scotia – a journey of some six hours (tel: 800-341 7981, www.marine-atlantic.ca). On the West Coast, the Victoria BC Clipper Ferry Service runs boats between Seattle and Victoria. It's a good idea to reserve passage well in advance for peak periods, tel: 250-382 8100 in Victoria, (206) 448-5000 in Seattle, toll-free 800-888 2535, www.clippervacations.com. Also on the West Coast, BC Ferries is the main carrier, www.bcferries.com or tel: 888-223 3779 in BC or 250-386 3431 from outside the province.

By road. Travel from the US to Montréal is via US Highways 87, 89 or 91. If you're heading for Toronto, follow the Queen Elizabeth Way from Niagara Falls, or Highway 401 (Macdonald-Cartier Freeway) from Detroit; US Interstate 5 leads to Seattle and the Canadian border. From there, it's just half-an-hour's drive into Vancouver on Canadian Highway 99. Maps that outline other points of entry to Canada from the US can be obtained from a company called MapArt which specialises in all maps of Canada, printed and digital (tel: 905-436 2525, www.mapart.com).

GUIDES AND TOURS

A visitor to Canada has many options to consider, including the following Canadian tour companies: WestJet Vacations, tel: 888-581 9499, or 403-444 2586, www.westjetvacations.com; Insight Vacations, email: info@insightvacations.ca, www.insightvacations.com; and Trafalgar, tel: 800-387 2680 or 416-322 8468, www. trafalgar.com. In BC, Talking Totem Tours specialise in self-guided tour packages to places where the First Nations of British Columbia gather and celebrate: tel: 250-444 7077, www.talking totemtours.com.

H

HEALTH AND MEDICAL CARE

Large hotels will have a contact number for a doctor or nurse. You can also seek treatment for minor complaints at medical centres in many cities. Hospital care in Canada is of a very high standard, and casualty departments generally give swift and efficient service. But medical fees can be costly, so make sure your travel or health insurance will cover you while in Canada. In an emergency, call 911 for assistance.

L

LANGUAGE

French and English are the two official languages. Canadian English largely resembles American English. In Québec, Canada's Francophone province, people appreciate your attempts to speak French, even if it's a simple *bonjour* or *merci*.

M

MEDIA

Newspapers and Magazines. The *National Post* and *The Globe and Mail* are distributed throughout Canada. *La Presse* is the ranking Québec daily. Larger bookstores and newsstands sell major American, British and French newspapers and magazines. Canada's largest news magazine, *Maclean's*, is published weekly.

Radio and Television. The Canadian Broadcasting Company (CBC) operates two nationwide television networks (French and English), along with an all-news network. CTV Global broadcasts two others. Regional and provincial networks, along with independent and US broadcasters, account for the rest.

CBC operates a national radio network, both AM and FM, In English and French. There are hundreds of private stations that fill the airwaves with news and music.

MONEY

The Canadian and US dollars have a different rate of exchange. All dollar prices quoted in this book are in Canadian dollars. Current coinage comprises: 1cent (a penny), 5 cents (a nickel), 10 cents (a dime), 25 cents (a quarter), $1 (a loonie), and $2 (a toonie). Bank notes come as $5, $10, $20, $50 and $100.

To get the best rate, exchange your money before leaving home. Canadian banks and foreign exchange bureaux will convert funds for a fee. US funds are readily accepted by many department stores and hotels, but may not offer the most advantageous rate.

O

OPENING TIMES

Standard business hours for stores are 10am–6pm, or 9pm in many larger cities. Stores in many parts of the country are open for more limited hours on Sunday. Drug and convenience stores generally close at 11pm but some operate for 24 hours. The majority of banks now open long hours, which may include Saturday, and also, in some instances, Sunday. Bank machines are readily available.

P

POLICE

The Royal Canadian Mounted Police (RCMP) is Canada's national police force. It operates in Canada's north and across Canada with the exception of Newfoundland and Labrador, Ontario and Québec, which each have their own provincial police forces: the Royal Newfoundland Constabulary, the Ontario Provincial Police, and La Sûreté du Québec. Many Canadian cities, large and small, also have their own municipally-funded police service. Should you need to contact the police, in any part of the country, phone 911.

POST OFFICES

Canada's post offices are open Monday to Friday during business hours, and sometimes on Saturday.

PUBLIC HOLIDAYS

When a holiday falls on a Sunday, the following day is often observed as the holiday. These are the official holidays, when all government offices and most businesses are closed:

New Year's Day	1 January
Good Friday	Friday before Easter
Victoria Day	Monday before 24 May
Canada Day	1 July
Labour Day	1st Monday in September
Thanksgiving	2nd Monday in October
Remembrance Day	11 November (banks, schools and government offices only)

Christmas	25 December
Boxing Day	26 December
St Patrick's Day (Newfoundland and Labrador)	17 March or the preceding Monday
St George's Day (Newfoundland and Labrador)	23 April or the preceding Monday
Discovery Day (Newfoundland and Labrador)	Monday closest to 24 June
Orangemens' Day (Newfoundland and Labrador)	Monday before 12 July
Civic Holiday (Alberta, British Columbia, Manitoba, New Brunswick, Northwest Territories, Nova Scotia, Ontario, Saskatchewan)	1st Monday in August
Discovery Day (Yukon)	3rd Monday in August

T

TELEPHONES

The telephone system in Canada is similar to that in the US. Payphone costs begin at 50 cents, but they can be hard to find. For collect or other operator-assisted calls, dial '0' then the number you wish to reach.

Dial '1' (Ottawa +613, Montréal +514 or +438, Vancouver +604 or +778, Victoria +250, Winnipeg +204, Toronto +416 or +647, Québec City +418, Calgary +403 or +587, Edmonton +780 or +587, Halifax +902, St. John's +709) for long-distance calls charged to the originating phone.

Mobile phones: Some US providers include Canada within their area of service, and others allow you to buy a service package for your trip that eliminates or reduces roaming charges. Visitors coming from places other than the US should purchase a pre-paid Canada SIM card which generally requires a SIM-unlocked cell GSM cell phone that supports the 1900 frequency.

TIME ZONES

Canada divides into six zones: Newfoundland Standard Time, NST (GMT –3½); Atlantic, AST (GMT –4); Eastern, EST (GMT –5); Central, CST (GMT –6); Mountain, MST (GMT –7); and Pacific, PST (GMT –8). Daylight Saving Time is from the second Sunday in March, when the clocks go forward an hour, until the first Sunday in November, when they revert to standard time (except in most of Saskatchewan, eastern areas of Quebec, and small pockets of Ontario and BC where clocks do not change).

TIPPING

Airport/hotel porter, per bag	$1
Maid, per day	$2
Waiter	15 percent
Taxi driver	10–15 percent
Tour guide	10 percent

TOILETS

'Restroom', 'washroom' or 'lavatory' will all be understood in Canada. In Québec, you may encounter *Hommes* (Men) and *Dames* (Ladies), though they are usually marked with pictographs.

TOURIST INFORMATION

The main office of the **Canadian Tourism Commission** is located at: Suite 1400, Four Bentall Centre, 1055 Dunsmuir Street, Box 49230, Vancouver, BC V7X 1L2, tel: 604-638 8300; www.canada tourism.com.

Each province also has its own tourism organisation:

Alberta: Travel Alberta, PO Box 2500, Edmonton, AB, T5J 2Z4; tel: 1-800-252 3782 in North America and 780-427 4321 outside North America; www.travelalberta.com.

British Columbia: Tourism British Columbia, 510 Burrard Street, 12th Floor, Vancouver, BC, V6Z 3A8; tel: 1-800-435 5622; overseas callers tel: 250-387 1642; www.hellobc.com.

Manitoba: Travel Manitoba, 7th Floor, 155 Carlton Street, Winnipeg, MB, R3C 3H8; tel: 1-800-665 0040 or 204-927 7838 outside North America; www.travelmanitoba.com.

New Brunswick: Tourism New Brunswick, PO Box 12345, Campbellton, NB, E3N 3T6; tel: 1-800-561 0123; www.tourismnew brunswick.ca.

Newfoundland and Labrador: Newfoundland and Labrador Tourism, PO Box 8700, St John's, NL A1B 4J6; tel: 1-800-563 6353 or 1-709-729 2830 outside North America; www.newfoundland labrador.com.

Northwest Territories: NWT Tourism, Box 610, Yellowknife, NT, X1A 2N5; tel: 1-800-661 0788 or 1-867-873 7200 outside North America; www.spectacularnwt.com.

Nova Scotia: Nova Scotia Department of Tourism and Culture, PO Box 456, Halifax, Nova Scotia, B3J 2R5; tel: 1-800-565 0000, or for local calls and outside North America 1-902-425 5781; www. novascotia.com.

Nunavut: Nunavut Tourism, Box 1450, Iqaluit, NU, X0A 0H0; tel: 1-866-686 2888 or 867-979 4636 outside North America; www. nunavuttourism.com.

Ontario: Ontario Tourism Marketing Partnership Corporation, 10 Dundas Street East, Suite 900 Toronto, Ontario, Canada M7A 2A1; tel: 1-800-668 2746; www.ontariotravel.net.

Prince Edward Island: Tourism PEI, tel: 800-463 4734 or, outside North America, 1-902-368-4444; www.gov.pe.ca/visitorsguide.

Québec: Tourisme Québec, C.P. 979, Montréal, PQ, H3C 2W3; tel: 1-877-266 5687; www.bonjourquebec.com.

Saskatchewan: Tourism Saskatchewan, 189-1621 Albert Street, Regina, SK S4P 2S5; tel: 1-877-237 2273; www.sasktourism.com.

Yukon: Yukon Department of Tourism and Culture, PO Box 2703, Whitehorse, YK, Y1A 2C6; tel: 1-800-661 0494; www.travel yukon.com.

TRANSPORT

By car. Most cities and large towns lie on or near the Trans-Canada Highway, the country's main east–west artery. It crosses southern Canada from Newfoundland to Victoria on the Pacific, a distance of 7,821km (4,860 miles). The going is slower in the rural north, where roads may be unpaved.

By air. Canada has two national airlines and many more regional and local carriers. Frequent scheduled and charter flights connect the cities and larger towns, while light planes provide regular service to places that are inaccessible by road. Seaplanes shuttle between coastal towns and offshore islands.

By bus. Greyhound routes cover Canada from coast to coast, and many regional companies cooperate to provide convenient countrywide connections. Stopovers may be made on most lines, and passes for cheap travel during specified periods may be available. Greyhound's Discovery Pass is valid for certain routes into Canada.

By train. Cross the country by train (travel time: five days), or take a series of short, scenic journeys – up into the Arctic on the Polar Bear Express, for example. It's essential to book well ahead for these routes during the tourist season. The national company is VIA Rail. Several smaller lines operate regional services: the Ontario Northland, Algoma Central and the Rocky Mountaineer. Long-distance trains have observation, dining and sleeping cars (with berths, roomettes and bedrooms).

By boat. Car and passenger ferries shuttle year-round between the mainland and offshore islands. Ferries also serve central Canada's lakes and rivers. Two popular routes are BC Ferries' Port Hardy to Prince Rupert run by way of the magnificent Inside Passage, or the spectacular crossing on the Manitoulin Island Ferry from Tobermory to Manitoulin Island in Lake Huron. A replica steamship plies the St Lawrence River between Kingston and Québec City, and the nostalgic *Paddlewheel Queen* and *Paddlewheel Princess* cruise Manitoba's Red River. You can even sail Hudson Bay on a tour or charter boat.

Local transport. You'll have no problem getting around the cities on public transport, via the underground (subway), bus, tram or trolleybus. The newest thing in Canadian rapid transit is the light railway. Toronto, Edmonton, Calgary and Vancouver, among other cities, have introduced this system.

Subway tickets or tokens may be purchased singly or in sets, at newsstands or in stations. When you board a city bus in Canada, have the exact fare ready. Drivers never carry change. Get a transfer if you need to connect to another line.

Taxis wait for customers at airports, railway stations and hotels. Hail a cab in the street or ask for one by telephone (look in the *Yellow Pages* under Taxicabs). A 10–15 percent tip is customary.

V

VISAS AND ENTRY REQUIREMENTS

US citizens travelling by air between the US and Canada must present a current passport. Amtrak also requires a current passport if travelling by rail between the US and Canada. Permanent residents in the US must bring their green card. For most updated information visit the Citizenship and Immigration Canada website at www.cic.gc.ca/english/visit/visas.asp.

All physical importation and exportation of currency and monetary instruments equal to or greater than $10,000 must be reported to Canada Customs, tel: 800-461 9999 in Canada and 506-636 5064 or 204-983 3500 outside of Canada. You can also access information at www.cbsa-asfc.gc.ca/noncan-eng.html.

W

WEBSITES

There a number of websites with useful, up-to-date information. In addition to the sites listed below, see Tourist Information *(page 247)* for the official national and provincial tourism websites.

www.ago.net Art Gallery of Ontario

www.cntower.ca CN Tower, Toronto

www.glenbow.org Glenbow Museum

www.theglobeandmail.com Globe and Mail newspaper

www.hhof.com Hockey Hall of Fame

www.museum.gov.ns.ca/mma Maritime Museum of the Atlantic

www.musee-mccord.qc.ca McCord Museum

www.macm.org Museum of Contemporary Art

www.nac-cna.ca National Arts Centre

www.gallery.ca/en National Gallery of Canada

www.therooms.ca The Rooms Provincial Museum, Newfoundland

www.pc.gc.ca Parks Canada

www.rcmpheritagecentre.com RCMP Heritage Centre

www.rockymountaineer.com Rocky Mountaineer Railtours

www.stlc.com St Lawrence Centre for the Arts, Toronto

www.torontoharbour.com Toronto Harbour

WEIGHTS AND MEASURES

Canada uses the metric system for most measurements.

Y

YOUTH HOSTELS

Youth accommodation. For a complete list of Canadian hostels, contact Hostelling International Canada, www.hihostels.ca or tel: 613-237 7884 for the hostel booking centre that you require. Non-members can usually stay at a hostel if there is room, on payment of a small surcharge. During the summer, some Canadian universities and colleges offer rooms in their residences. Tourist offices can provide addresses. Alternatively, you should be able to find a YMCA at www.ymca.ca or, for women, a YWCA at www.ywca.ca for short-term accommodation. Single or double rooms are the norm.

INDEX

Berlitz pocket guide

Canada

Tenth Edition 2012
Reprinted 2013

Written by Jack Altman
Updated by Joanna Ebbutt
Edited by Paula Soper
Series Editor: Tom Stainer

Photography credits
Alamy 153; Calgary 12; Canada Tourism Commission 214; Natalia Bratslavsky/Fotolia.com 2T, 186; Elenathewise/Fotolia.com 149, 150; Jackie Garrow/APA 106, 109, 123, 130, 132, 173, 176, 181–185, 191, 198, 225; Image Ontario 4-5, 67, 68, 80; iStockphoto 5TL, 6TL, 40, 58, 63, 70, 78, 104, 141, 179, 201; C. Kreignoff /Archives Canada 26; Manitoba Tourism 209; Mary Evans 29, 31; Montreal Tourism 85, 220; Musée des Beaux-Arts de Montréal 97; Musée d'art contemporain de Montréal 107; New Brunswick Images 145; Team Nowitz /APA 3CR, 4TL, 6C, 13, 89–96, 99, 101, 102, 104, 111–120, 226; Nova Scotia Tourism 8, 124, 126, 127, 129, 131, 135, 139, 146; Ontario Archives 32; Ontario Tourism 14; Ottawa Tourist Board 5BR, 11, 48, 73, 74, 76, 81; D.Plummer 15, 142, 223; Sakatchewan Tourism 4BL, 4TL, 189, 192, 195, 196, 197, 206, 210, 215; Sapeo/Fotolia.com 108; N Sumner 37, 136; Tim Thompson 2BR, 5TR, 7C, 7T, 10, 42, 44, 51,54, 56, 57, 154–171, 175, 188, 212, 229; Vancouver playhouse 219; Yukon Tourism 203, 204. **Cover:** Corbis

Contact us

At Berlitz we strive to keep our guides as accurate and up to date as possible, but if you find anything that has changed, or if you have any suggestions on ways to improve this guide, then we would be delighted to hear from you. Berlitz Publishing, PO Box 7910, London SE1 1WE, England.
email: berlitz@apaguide.co.uk
www.insightguides.com/berlitz